CRAFT
PIZZA

CRAFT PIZZA

HOMEMADE CLASSIC, SICILIAN AND SOURDOUGH PIZZA, CALZONE AND FOCACCIA

MAXINE CLARK

RYLAND PETERS & SMALL
LONDON • NEW YORK

For my brother Paul (1961–2015), who had a Eureka moment eating a pizza in Naples.

Senior Designer Toni Kay
Commissioning Editor Stephanie Milner
Production Mai-Ling Collyer
Art Director Leslie Harrington
Editorial Director Julia Charles
Publisher Cindy Richards
Food Stylist Maxine Clark and Emily Kydd
Assistant Food Stylists Lizzie Harris, Susie Plant and Jo Lee
Prop Stylist Róisín Nield
Indexer Vanessa Bird

Author's Acknowledgments

My thanks go to editors Julia, Rachel, Stephanie and Céline
at RPS who all worked on the book; art director and designer
Steve for his keen eye and keener taste buds; photographer
Richard Jung for his calmness while his studio was dusted in
a cloud of flour, and for really beautiful emotive photographs.
Thanks to Róisín for once again finding incredible atmospheric
props and backgrounds; Lizzie Harris, Susie Plant, and Jo
Lee for help with mixing, kneading, patting, and shopping.
Thanks also go to designer Toni Kay, photographer Mowie Kay,
prop stylist and food stylist Emily Kydd for their work on the
beautiful new images for this edition.

First published in 2016
This revised edition published in 2020
by Ryland Peters & Small
20–21 Jockey's Fields, London WC1R 4BW
and
341 E 116th St, New York NY 10029
www.rylandpeters.com

10 9 8 7 6

Some recipes in this book were previously published in
Pizza, Calzone & Focaccia by Maxine Clark in 2007.

Text © Maxine Clark 2016, 2020
Design and photographs © Ryland Peters & Small 2016, 2020
For full photography credits, see page 159.

ISBN: 978-1-78879-194-6

Printed in China

Notes

• Both British (Metric) and American (Imperial plus US cups)
measurements are included in these recipes for convenience,
however it is important to work with one set of measurements
and not alternate between the two within a recipe.

• All spoon measurements are level unless otherwise specified.

• All eggs are large (UK) or extra-large (US), unless specified
as large, in which case US extra-large should be used.
Uncooked or partially cooked eggs should not be served to the
very old, frail, young children, pregnant women or those with
compromised immune systems.

• Ovens should be preheated to the specified
temperatures. We recommend using an
oven thermometer. If using a fan-assisted
oven, adjust temperatures according to
the manufacturer's instructions.

• When a recipe calls for the grated zest
of citrus fruit, buy unwaxed fruit and
wash well before using. If you can only
find treated fruit, scrub well in warm
soapy water before using.

• Whenever butter is called for within
these recipes, unsalted butter should
be used.

MIX
Paper from
responsible sources
FSC® C106563
www.fsc.org

CONTENTS

INTRODUCTION

I was bitten by the pizza bug in the best of all places, a huge farmhouse kitchen in Tuscany. I was working with chef Alvaro Maccioni teaching Italian cookery classes, when we discovered that a huge bread or pizza oven was hidden behind a small, blackened iron door. Aristide, the old man who swept and set the huge fires in the lodge, set and lit the oven, first with faggots of fine chestnut branches to quickly warm the porous base and domed brick roof, changing to metre-long, thinnish logs of seasoned hardwood to sustain the heat and create a bed of wood coals over the base. After a few hours it was ready. The live coals were swept to one side in a pile, the base or sole of the oven swept clean with a wet brush and another log or two placed on top of the coals to maintain the heat.

During this time, we had mixed and energetically kneaded dough, shaped it into balls and set them on a huge wooden tray, dusting the tops copiously with flour. The dough rose easily on that chilly October day, as the heat from the now roaring fire-pit of the oven was tremendous. The balls rose and cracked their floury caps. These were upturned and patted or rolled out, toppings added and, in turn, guided by Alvaro or twinkly-eyed Aristide, everyone slipped their pizza onto the *pala* or pizza peel and shot it into the oven. Five minutes later we were munching on what was voted 'the best pizza in the world' and sipping ice-cold beer.

Since then, I have fired up different sizes and types of ovens both at home and in Italy, and made countless pizzas, learning more with every dough made and every pizza patted. I have tried to make the recipes in this book home-oven friendly, as I am well aware that most people will not have a wood-fired oven or indeed the time required to fire it up. Good pizza can be made at home, as long as the dough is soft and pillowy, the oven is hot and there's a heavy baking sheet or bakestone inside. The taste of the wood smoke won't be there, but the pizza will bake with a nice chewy crust. Most importantly, the ingredients must be the best and freshest – there's no room for kitchen leftovers.

Pizza is said to have originated on the streets of Naples, to feed and fill ordinary working people cheaply. Its roots are distinctly southern Italian and pizza is considered a food of the city. Pizza alla Napoletana is always 'open pizza' (never filled, folded and baked). However, the way to eat pizza in the street is to fold it in quarters, hold it in a napkin and munch it like a sandwich. The Associazione Verace Pizza Napoletana lays down strict rules for the making and cooking of pizza in order to be able to sell it as 'Pizza Napoletana'. Little stuffed and deep-fried *pizzelle* and *panzerotti* are other examples of street food from Naples and Campania. In Rome, pizza is sold by the metre (or its parts). Throughout Italy, other types of flat hearth breads, such as focaccia and schiacciata, were traditionally made at home on the hot hearth where the embers had been.

The only ingredients necessary to make pizza dough are flour, salt, yeast and water. I like to add olive oil as it gives a good texture and flavour to the dough when baked at home. Salt will bring the flavour out of the dough and strengthen the crust but if you are using a flaky sea or crystal salt, make sure it is finely ground or dissolve it in the warm water before adding it to the flour. Any type of yeast you are happy with will do – just follow the manufacturer's instructions, using the liquid specified in the recipe. As for water, the softer the water, the better the dough, so I would use filtered water or even bottled water in hard-water areas. Other breads, like focaccia, rely on olive oil for flavour, so you must use extra virgin olive oil. It doesn't have to be an expensive one – a supermarket blend of extra virgin olive oils will do. Always anoint your piping hot pizza with extra virgin olive oil (flavoured or not) before you eat it. Not only will it look better, it will taste sublime!

My final advice to any novice pizza-maker is to keep the choice of topping as simple as you can to truly appreciate the flavours. The crust is all-important and turns soggy if it is weighed down too much. Slice meat and vegetables thinly and don't smother the base with sauce or cheese. Most important of all, eat it hot, hot, hot, straight out of the oven. I hope you enjoy using this book – I cooked every one of the pizzas for the photographs and we never tired of eating them at the studio or at home as they were all so different from each other that there was always something new to taste. Go on, get your hands in some dough right now and bake a fragrant pizza. You don't need any special ingredients – just start off with an olive oil, salt and garlic topping and savour your first real pizza.

BASICS EQUIPMENT AND UTENSILS

Making pizza dough couldn't be easier and when you become familiar with the process, you can guess the quantities by eye. To make really good pizza, you will need a few basic items in the kitchen, the most important being your hands!

You should have a good selection of the usual suspects: **mixing bowls**, **measuring spoons**, **measuring cups**, **weighing scales**; a good **sharp knife** or **pastry wheel** for cutting dough; a **large serrated knife** for cutting focaccia.

My favourite gadget is a **pastry scraper** which can be used as a knife, scoop and board scraper or cleaner. Scrapers come in all guises but they usually comprise a rectangular metal 'blade,' one edge of which is covered by a wooden or plastic handle that fits into the palm of your hand.

If you are really serious about pizza-making and want to make dough in quantity, an **electric food mixer** will take the pain out of mixing and kneading large batches of dough, although there's nothing quite as satisfying as hand-kneading a big, soft pillow of dough.

Clingfilm/plastic wrap is the modern alternative to a damp kitchen towel. This is used to cover a dough when it is rising to keep it moist and to stop the surface drying out and forming a crust, which can impair the rising. Clingfilm/plastic wrap on its own will stick to a dough, so either lightly rub the dough with a little olive oil or spray or brush the clingfilm/plastic wrap lightly with oil before covering the dough. Alternatively, you can cover the rising dough with a large, upturned mixing bowl.

Baking parchment is a revelation for making pizza. There is no need to dust the bottom of the pizza with masses of extra flour (which never cooks) to prevent it sticking. Dusting with cornmeal is in no way authentic and it sticks to the dough, ruining the texture.

A **good, steady work surface** at the right height is essential for energetic kneading. The surface should be able to cope with sticky dough, flour and olive oil and should be easy to clean.

A **flour sifter** or **shaker** is useful as it will limit the flour you sprinkle onto the dough and is always to hand. Alternatively, you can make do with a little bowl of extra flour on the side, for dusting.

An **olive-oil pourer** will allow you to drizzle small amounts of olive oil onto a pizza or into a dough. Some are cans with long spouts and some neatly fit into the olive-oil bottle itself.

A **water spray** mists a dough with just enough water to keep it moist.

Pastry brushes are always handy in a kitchen for brushing the tops of calzone with oil or water and the edges of dough with water before sealing.

Cookie cutters will cut dough into smaller shapes for stuffing or filling.

You will need one or two **deep, heavy round metal pans/pizza pans/springform cake pans** for deep-pan pizzas and focaccias; **heavy rectangular pans** and **baking sheets** with sides for larger pizzas; and good,

nicely. There are all types from round to rectangular on the market – some ovens have them as an optional extra. Thick, unglazed quarry/terracotta tiles are a good alternative – use them to line a shelf in the oven. They can be any size, as long as they fit together.

Having tested and cooked all sorts of doughs in all types of ovens, I have found that pizza cooks best in a **standard electric oven** which can reach temperatures of more than 200°C (400°F) Gas 6 and ideally, 220°C (425°F) Gas 7. This will cook the base quickly and be as close to the real thing as possible. Although convection ovens will work for pizza- and focaccia-baking, they tend to dry out the crust before it browns and the crust can be very pale.

A **wood-burning oven** is the ultimate for the truly serious pizza aficionado. One of these will heat to the right temperature and give that all-important smoky taste to the pizza, which comes from the burning wood. A pizza cooked in one of these will take just minutes as the temperature is more than 500°C (930°F). Domestic ovens are available (page 158) and could end up being your new best friend!

heavy, rimless **baking sheets** (or turn them upside down) for baking pizzas and to act as pizza peels or paddles to shoot the pizza into the oven. Pans with a nonstick surface tend to 'stew' doughs – I prefer metal, iron or heavy aluminium. Never use the large pans with perforated bases to make fresh pizzas – these are specifically for reheating bought pizzas and do not work with fresh dough.

Pizza peels or **paddles** are a luxury, but lovely to have and very functional. Wooden peels can act as a serving dish. Metal peels are more practical, although they heat up when they are repeatedly going in and out of the oven can make the dough stick to them.

Pizza wheels slice efficiently through a hot pizza without dragging off all the topping.

A **'testo'** or **baking stone** is an affordable luxury if you don't have that outdoor, wood-fired pizza oven. Preheated in the oven for at least 30 minutes before starting to bake, the stone mimics the base of a real pizza oven and when the uncooked pizza comes into contact with the stone, the moisture is absorbed, the heat evenly distributed and the base will crisp up

PIZZA POINTERS

Yeast

Whatever yeast you use, it needs moisture and warmth to develop. Make sure the liquid is at the correct temperature – too cold and the dough will rise slowly; too hot and you risk killing the yeast. When a recipe states 'hand-hot water,' it should be between 40.5°C (105°F) and 46°C (115°F).

Flour

For pizza, using fine Italian 'O' grade flour or unbleached plain/all-purpose flour gives the best crust at home. For focaccia, Italian '00' flour or cake flour gives the best domestic results. If you are making dough in a hurry, warm the flour in the microwave for 10 seconds before adding the other ingredients. Always have surplus flour on hand to dust your dough, hands, rolling pin and work surface.

Dough

When making the dough, remember: the wetter the dough, the better the dough. A stiff, firm dough is difficult to knead and even more difficult to shape. It will have a poor texture and will not rise properly. If kneaded well, the stickiness soon disappears. Always have surplus olive oil on hand for oiling clingfilm/plastic wrap, dough, bowls and baking pans, when required, to stop the dough from sticking.

Kneading

If the dough sticks to your hands when kneading, stop and quickly wash your hands then dip them in a little flour to dry them. You will find the dough doesn't stick to clean hands. Kneading should stretch the dough and develop the elastic gluten in the flour – don't be shy in pulling and stretching the dough.

Shaping

Starting with a perfect round ball makes it easy to stretch the dough into a circle. Shape each one into a smooth ball and place on a floured kitchen towel to rise. Dredge liberally all over with flour. When risen, flip the balls over onto a work surface (the flour will have stuck to the dough giving it a non-stick base) and roll out.

Topping

The cardinal sin in pizza-making is to overwhelm perfectly made dough with too much topping. This can make it difficult to shoot it into the oven and will prevent it rising. If any topping drips down the side of the pizza making it wet, it will not rise. Cheese that misses the target will glue the pizza to the baking stone or parchment.

Crust

If you like pizza with a good crisp crust and make them often, it is worth investing in a porous 'testo' or baking stone. Some ovens have them as an accessory, but they are cheap to buy. Otherwise a large, heavy baking sheet that will not warp will do.

Baking

The best way to get a pizza into the oven is to roll the dough directly onto baking parchment and slide this onto a rimless baking sheet or pizza peel. It will then slide onto the preheated 'testo' or baking sheet easily. For the best results, quickly slide out the baking parchment from under the pizza 5 minutes after the pizza has set to make sure that the crust crisps up.

Serving

Always serve open pizza as soon as it is cooked, slip it onto a wooden board and cut it using a pizza wheel, as knives can drag the topping. Leave filled pizzas to cool for 5 minutes before eating as they can burn the mouth!

Eating

Pizza is best eaten in the hand – the crust is there to act as a handle! In Naples, pizzas are folded in four and eaten like a huge sandwich in a paper napkin. Using a knife and fork just sends it skimming across the plate!

Basic Pizza Dough

This will make the typical Neapolitan pizza – soft and chewy with a crisp crust or *cornicione*.

25 g/1 cake compressed yeast,
1 tablespoon/1 packet active dry yeast,
or 2 teaspoons fast-action dried yeast

½ teaspoon sugar

250 ml/1 cup hand-hot water

500 g/4 cups Italian '0' or '00' flour
or unbleached plain/all-purpose flour,
plus extra to dust

1 teaspoon fine sea salt

1 tablespoon olive oil

**MAKES 2 MEDIUM-CRUST
PIZZA BASES**
(25–30 CM/10–12 INCHES)

In a medium bowl, cream the compressed yeast with the sugar and beat in the hand-hot water. Leave for 10 minutes until frothy. For other yeasts, follow the manufacturer's instructions.

Sift the flour and salt into a large bowl and make a well in the centre. Pour in the yeast mixture, then the olive oil. Mix together with a round-bladed knife, then use your hands until the dough comes together. Tip out onto a lightly floured surface, wash and dry your hands, then knead briskly for 5–10 minutes until smooth, shiny and elastic. (5 minutes for warm hands, 10 minutes for cold hands!) Don't add extra flour – a wetter dough is better. If you feel the dough is sticky, flour your hands, not the dough. The dough should be quite soft. If it is *really* too soft, knead in a little more flour.

To test if the dough is ready, roll it into a fat sausage, take each end in either hand, lift the dough up and stretch the dough outward, gently wiggling it up and down – it should stretch out quite easily. If it doesn't, it needs more kneading. Shape the dough into a neat ball. Put in an oiled bowl, cover with clingfilm/plastic wrap or a damp kitchen towel and let rise in a warm, draught-free place until doubled in size – about 1½ hours.

Uncover the dough, punch out the air, then tip out onto a lightly floured work surface. Divide into 2 and shape into smooth balls. Place the balls well apart on baking parchment, cover loosely with clingfilm/plastic wrap and let rise for 1–1½ hours. Use as desired.

BASIC SOURDOUGH PIZZA BASE

Sourdough starters need a lot of love and attention, so I felt that a quick, no-nonsense recipe was needed for a sourdough pizza. This follows the same lines as Basic Pizza Dough (page 12) and you do NOT require a starter... the secret is in the sourdough breadcrumbs!

25 g/1 cake compressed yeast,
1 tablespoon/1 packet active dry yeast,
or 2 teaspoons fast-action dried yeast

½ teaspoon sugar

250 ml/1 cup hand-hot water

400 g/3 cups unbleached white bread flour, 50 g/scant ½ cup rye flour, 50 g/1 cup fresh or stale sourdough breadcrumbs, plus extra flour to dust

1 teaspoon fine sea salt

1 tablespoon olive oil

**MAKES 2 MEDIUM-CRUST PIZZA BASES
(25–30 CM/10–12 INCHES)**

In a medium bowl, cream the fresh yeast with the sugar and whisk in the hand-hot water. Leave for 10 minutes until frothy. For other yeasts, follow the manufacturer's instructions.

Sift the flours and salt into a large bowl, stir in the breadcrumbs and make a well in the centre. Pour in the yeast mixture, then the olive oil. Mix together with a round-bladed knife, then use your hands until the dough comes together. Tip out onto a lightly floured surface, wash and dry your hands, then knead briskly for 5–10 minutes until smooth, shiny and elastic. (5 minutes for warm hands, 10 minutes for cold hands!) Don't add extra flour at this stage – a wetter dough is better. If you feel the dough is sticky, flour your hands, not the dough. The dough should be quite soft. If it is really too soft, knead in a little more flour.

To test if the dough is ready, roll it into a fat sausage, take each end in either hand, lift the dough up and stretch the dough outwards, gently wiggling it up and down – it should stretch out quite easily. If it doesn't, it needs more kneading.

Shape the dough into a neat ball. Put in an oiled bowl, cover with clingfilm/plastic wrap or a damp tea towel and leave to rise in a warm, draught-free place until doubled in size – about 1½ hours (or overnight in the fridge for a stronger flavour).

Uncover the dough, punch out the air, then tip out onto a lightly floured work surface. Divide into 2 and shape into smooth balls. Place the balls well apart on non-stick baking parchment, cover loosely with clingfilm/plastic wrap and leave to rise for 1–1½ hours. Use as desired.

SICILIAN PIZZA DOUGH

10 g/½ cake compressed yeast,
1 teaspoon/½ packet active dry yeast,
or ½ teaspoon fast-action dried yeast

a pinch of sugar

150 ml/⅔ cup hand-hot water

250 g/2 cups fine semolina flour
(*farina di semola*) or durum wheat flour

½ teaspoon fine sea salt

1 tablespoon olive oil

1 tablespoon freshly squeezed
lemon juice

**MAKES 2 THIN-CRUST PIZZA
BASES** (8–10 CM/3¼–4 INCHES)

Sicilians tend to use the indigenous yellow *farina di semola* (hard wheat flour), which ensures a lighter crust, with lemon juice to add to the lightness and strengthen the dough.

In a medium bowl, cream the compressed yeast with the sugar and beat in the hand-hot water. Leave for 10 minutes until frothy. For other yeasts, follow the manufacturer's instructions.

Sift the flour and salt into a large bowl and make a well in the centre. Pour in the yeast mixture, olive oil and lemon juice. Mix until the dough comes together. Add more water if necessary – the dough should be very soft.
Tip out onto a lightly floured surface, wash and dry your hands, then knead briskly for at least 10 minutes until smooth, shiny and elastic. It takes longer to knead this type of dough. Don't add extra flour – a wetter dough is better. If you feel the dough is sticky, flour your hands, not the dough. The dough should be quite soft. If it is really too soft, knead in a little more flour.

To test if the dough is ready, roll it into a fat sausage, take each end in either hand, lift the dough up and stretch the dough outward, gently wiggling it up and down – it should stretch out quite easily. If it doesn't, it needs more kneading. Shape the dough into a neat ball. Put in an oiled bowl, cover with clingfilm/plastic wrap or a damp kitchen towel and leave to rise in a warm, draught-free place until doubled in size – about 1½ hours.

Uncover the dough, punch out the air, then tip out onto a lightly floured work surface. Divide into 2 and shape into smooth balls. Put the balls well apart on baking parchment, cover loosely with clingfilm/plastic wrap and let rise for 1–1½ hours. Use as desired.

MAKING FOCACCIA

Focaccias are found in many different guises all over Italy and can be thin and crisp, thick and soft, round or square. I make this deep one in a round pan but it can be made in any shape you wish and cooked on a baking sheet. Although focaccia dough is softer and has a good deal of olive oil added to it, the mixing method is the same as pizza dough. Use the recipe for Deep-pan Focaccia on page 100, then follow the steps below to shape your bread.

Follow the recipe on page 100 so that the dough is at the stage where it has risen twice.

Uncover the dough. Push your fingertips into the dough right down to the base of the pan (don't overdo it!), to make deep dimples all over the surface. The dough will deflate slightly. Drizzle very generously with olive oil (about 80 ml/$\frac{1}{3}$ cup) so that the dimples contain little pools of delicious oil.

Top with little sprigs of rosemary leaves and a generous sprinkling of salt.

Re-cover with clingfilm/plastic wrap or a damp kitchen towel and leave the dough to rise to the top of the pans – about 30 minutes.

Resume the recipe on page 100.

PIZZAIOLA SAUCE

This is a key ingredient of pizza and gives it its distinctive flavour. It is a specialty of Naples, but is quite common throughout Italy. To acquire its concentrated, almost caramelized flavour, the tomatoes must be fried over a lively heat.

8 tablespoons/½ cup olive oil

2 garlic cloves, chopped

1 teaspoon dried oregano

2 x 400-g/14-oz. cans chopped tomatoes (drained and juice reserved) or 900 g/2 lbs. fresh tomatoes, halved and cored

sea salt and freshly ground black pepper

**MAKES ABOUT
400 ML/1¾ CUPS**

In a large shallow pan, heat the oil almost to smoking point (a wok is good for this).

Standing back to avoid the spluttering, add the garlic, oregano and tomatoes, then the reserved canned tomato juice (if using). Cook over a fierce heat for 5–8 minutes or until the sauce is thick and glossy. Season.

Pass the sauce through a food mill (*mouli*) set over a bowl, to remove seeds and skin. You can put the smooth sauce back in the pan to reduce further if you like. Ladle the sauce into the centre of the pizza crust and spread it out in a circular motion with the back of a ladle.

CLASSIC PESTO GENOVESE

Don't stint on the fresh basil here – it is instrumental in making this the most wonderful sauce in the world! Adding a little softened butter at the end gives the pesto a creaminess that will help it coat hot pasta. The texture is ideal when the pesto is pounded by hand, so try it once and you'll never make it in a food processor again! Pesto can be frozen successfully – some suggest leaving out the cheese and beating it in when the pesto has thawed, but I have never had any problems including it in the beginning.

2 garlic cloves

50 g/½ cup pine nuts

50 g/2 big handfuls fresh basil leaves

150 ml/⅔ cup extra virgin olive oil, plus extra to preserve

50 g/3 tablespoons unsalted butter, softened

4 tablespoons/¼ cup freshly grated Parmesan cheese

sea salt and freshly ground black pepper

**MAKES ABOUT
250 ML/1 CUP**

Peel the garlic and put it in a pestle and mortar with a little salt and the pine nuts. Pound until broken up. Add the basil leaves, a few at a time, pounding and mixing to a paste. Gradually beat in the olive oil, little by little, until the mixture is creamy and thick.

Alternatively, put everything in a food processor and process until just smooth.

Beat in the butter and season with pepper, then beat in the Parmesan. Spoon into a screw-top jar with a layer of olive oil on top to exclude the air, then refrigerate for up to 2 weeks, until needed.

FIERY RED PESTO

1 large red (bell) pepper

50 g/2 big handfuls fresh basil leaves

1 garlic clove

30 g/⅓ cup toasted pine nuts

6 sun-dried tomatoes in oil, drained

2 ripe tomatoes, skinned

3 tablespoons tomato purée/paste

½ teaspoon chilli/chili powder

50 g/½ cup freshly grated
Parmesan cheese

150 ml/⅔ cup olive oil,
plus extra to preserve

**MAKES ABOUT
350 ML/1½ CUPS**

Years ago, long before it appeared on supermarket shelves, I devised this recipe to remind me of the flavours of southern Italy. Needless to say, this tastes really special and you can adjust the heat to your liking. Although not at all Italian, coriander/cilantro is a fantastic alternative to the basil.

Preheat the grill/broiler to high.

Place the (bell) pepper on the grill/broiler rack and grill/broil, turning occasionally, until blackened all over. Put the (bell) pepper in a covered bowl until cool enough to handle, then peel off the skin. Halve and remove the core and seeds.

Place the (bell) pepper and the remaining ingredients, except the oil, in a food processor. Process until smooth, then, with the machine running, slowly add the oil. Spoon into a screw-top jar with a layer of olive oil on top to exclude the air, then refrigerate for up to 2 weeks, until needed.

BLACK OLIVE AND TOMATO RELISH

2 tablespoons sun-dried tomato oil

1 red onion, peeled and diced

1 garlic clove, peeled and crushed

5 sun-dried tomatoes in oil,
drained and diced

250 g/8 oz. pitted/stoned black
(or oven-dried) olives

1 fresh bay leaf

15 fresh basil leaves, torn into pieces

freshly squeezed juice of 1 lemon

3–4 tablespoons extra virgin olive oil,
plus extra to preserve

sea salt and freshly ground
black pepper

**MAKES ABOUT
350 ML/1½ CUPS**

This is a wonderfully useful relish to have sitting in the fridge to spread onto pizza dough or simply to serve with flatbreads as a dip. I always use the wrinkly, oven-dried black olives (sometimes known as Greek-style, but not Kalamata) as they have a good, rich flavour.

In a medium saucepan, heat the sun-dried tomato oil and gently sweat the onion and garlic for a few minutes. Add the sun-dried tomatoes, olives and bay leaf and continue to cook for a few minutes until the flavours have melded.

Season, remove from the heat and discard the bay leaf. Pour the mixture into a food processor with the basil and process until you have a coarse purée. (You may have to do this in 2 batches if there isn't enough room in the food processor.) Add the lemon juice, oil and more seasoning, if necessary.

Spoon into a screw-top jar with a layer of olive oil on top to exclude the air, then refrigerate for up to 2 weeks, until needed.

PIZZAS THICK AND THIN

PIZZA MARGHERITA

A Neapolitan baker called Raffaele Esposito is said to have been responsible for the birth of modern-day pizza. In 1889, in Naples, he baked three different pizzas for the visit of King Umberto I and Queen Margherita of Savoy. The Queen's favourite was very patriotic, symbolizing the flag of newly unified Italy in its colours of green (basil leaves), white (mozzarella) and red (tomatoes). It was then named Pizza Margherita in her honour and this is it. To be truly authentic, all the ingredients should be local – the basil should really be hand-picked from a Neapolitan balcony!

½ recipe Basic Pizza Dough (page 12), making just 1 ball of dough

3–4 tablespoons Pizzaiola Sauce (page 19)

50–75 g/2–3 oz. buffalo mozzarella or cow's milk mozzarella (*fior di latte*)

200 g/7 oz. very ripe cherry tomatoes, halved

a good handful of fresh basil leaves

extra virgin olive oil, to drizzle

sea salt and freshly ground black pepper

a testo, terracotta baking stone or a large, heavy baking sheet

a pizza peel or rimless baking sheet

MAKES 1 MEDIUM-CRUST PIZZA (25–35 CM/10–14 INCHES)

Put the testo, baking stone or a large, heavy baking sheet on the lower shelf of the oven. Preheat the oven to 220°C (425°F) Gas 7 for at least 30 minutes.

Lightly squeeze any excess moisture out of the mozzarella, then roughly slice it.

Uncover the dough, punch out the air and roll or pull into a 25-cm/10-inch circle directly onto baking parchment. Slide this onto the pizza peel or rimless baking sheet. Spread the pizzaiola sauce over the pizza crust, leaving a 1-cm/³/₈-inch rim around the edge. Scatter with the tomatoes and season.

Working quickly, open the oven door and slide paper and pizza onto the hot baking stone or baking sheet. If you are brave, try to shoot the pizza into the oven so that it leaves the paper behind – this takes practice!

Bake for 5 minutes, remove from the oven and scatter the mozzarella over the tomatoes. Return the pizza to the oven without the paper. Bake for a further 15 minutes or until the crust is golden and the cheese melted but still white. Remove from the oven, scatter with the basil leaves and drizzle with olive oil. Eat immediately.

Pizza Marinara

½ recipe Basic Pizza Dough (page 12), making just 1 ball of dough

3–4 tablespoons Pizzaiola Sauce (page 19)

200 g/2 or 3 very ripe tomatoes, sliced and seeded

2 garlic cloves, thinly sliced

1 teaspoon dried oregano

extra virgin olive oil, to drizzle

a few sprigs fresh oregano

sea salt and freshly ground black pepper

a testo, terracotta baking stone or a large, heavy baking sheet

a pizza peel or rimless baking sheet

MAKES 1 MEDIUM-CRUST PIZZA (25–35 CM/10–14 INCHES)

This is the classic pizza and it is always made without mozzarella. According to Neapolitans, when anchovies are added, it is transformed into a Pizza Romana. Dried oregano is preferable to fresh, as it is much more fragrant, especially if you crush it between your fingers before sprinkling over the pizza.

Put the testo, baking stone or a large, heavy baking sheet on the lower shelf of the oven. Preheat the oven to 220°C (425°F) Gas 7 for at least 30 minutes.

Uncover the dough, punch out the air and roll or pull into a 25-cm/10-inch circle directly onto baking parchment. Slide this onto the pizza peel or rimless baking sheet. Spread the pizzaiola sauce over the pizza crust, leaving a 1-cm/³/₈-inch rim around the edge. Scatter with the tomatoes and garlic, sprinkle with the dried oregano, drizzle with olive oil, then season.

Working quickly, open the oven door and slide paper and pizza onto the hot baking stone or baking sheet. If you are brave, try to shoot the pizza into the oven so that it leaves the paper behind – this takes practice!

Bake for 5 minutes, then carefully slide out the baking parchment. Bake the pizza for a further 15 minutes, or until the crust is golden. Remove from the oven, scatter with the fresh oregano and drizzle with olive oil. Eat immediately.

ANGRY PIZZA

Pizza arrabiata

½ recipe Basic Pizza Dough (page 12), making just 1 ball of dough

50–75 g/2–3 oz. buffalo mozzarella or cow's milk mozzarella (*fior di latte*)

200 g/6 plum tomatoes, halved

150 g/5 oz. fresh spicy sausage, sliced or removed from the skin and crumbled

50 g/2 oz. Peppadew or cherry peppers

½ teaspoon fennel seeds

dried chilli/hot red pepper flakes, to taste

chilli/chili oil or extra virgin olive oil, to drizzle

sea salt and freshly ground black pepper

a testo, terracotta baking stone or a large, heavy baking sheet

a pizza peel or rimless baking sheet

MAKES 1 MEDIUM-CRUST PIZZA (25–35 CM/10–14 INCHES)

This is quite a substantial pizza and can be as fiery and angry as you like – it's up to you how much chilli/chile you put in. I love this with fresh Italian sausage meat, but you could use thick slices of salame piccante or even a hot merguez or chorizo. Chilled beer is an essential accompaniment.

Put the testo, baking stone or a large, heavy baking sheet on the lower shelf of the oven. Preheat the oven to 220°C (425°F) Gas 7 for at least 30 minutes.

Lightly squeeze any excess moisture out of the mozzarella, then slice or chop into cubes.

Uncover the dough, punch out the air and roll or pull into a 25-cm/10-inch circle directly onto baking parchment. Slide this onto the pizza peel or rimless baking sheet.

Arrange the tomatoes over the pizza crust leaving a 1-cm/³/₈-inch rim around the edge. Scatter with the sausage, then the Peppadew peppers, then the mozzarella. Sprinkle with the fennel seeds and chilli/hot red pepper flakes, then season. Working quickly, open the oven door and slide paper and pizza onto the hot baking stone or baking sheet. If you are brave, try to shoot the pizza into the oven so that it leaves the paper behind – this takes practice!

Bake for 5 minutes, then slide out the baking parchment if possible. Bake for a further 15 minutes or until the crust is golden and the cheese melted but still white. Remove from the oven and drizzle with the chilli/chili oil. Eat immediately.

Pizza Bianca

Neapolitans naturally call pizza without tomatoes Pizza Bianca. All the flavour comes from the mozzarella, so this has to be the finest buffalo mozzarella. This cheese tends to be quite wet, so squeeze out any watery whey before slicing it. I like to add sage to the pizza – its muskiness beautifully complements the milky mozzarella.

½ recipe Basic Pizza Dough (page 12), making just 1 ball of dough

100 g/3½ oz. buffalo mozzarella or cow's milk mozzarella (*fior di latte*)

a handful of small fresh sage leaves

extra virgin olive oil, to drizzle

sea salt and freshly ground black pepper

a testo, terracotta baking stone or a large, heavy baking sheet

a pizza peel or rimless baking sheet

MAKES 1 MEDIUM-CRUST PIZZA (25–35 CM/10–14 INCHES)

Put the testo, baking stone or a large, heavy baking sheet on the lower shelf of the oven. Preheat the oven to 220°C (425°F) Gas 7 for at least 30 minutes.

Lightly squeeze any excess moisture out of the mozzarella, then slice it and leave the slices on paper towels for 5 minutes to absorb any remaining moisture.

Uncover the dough, punch out the air and roll or pull into a 25-cm/10-inch circle directly onto baking parchment. Slide this onto the pizza peel or rimless baking sheet. Arrange the mozzarella evenly over the pizza crust, leaving a 1-cm/³⁄₈-inch rim around the edge. Scatter the sage over the cheese, then season and drizzle with olive oil.

Working quickly, open the oven door and slide paper and pizza onto the hot baking stone or baking sheet. If you are brave, try to shoot the pizza into the oven so that it leaves the paper behind – this takes practice!

Bake for 5 minutes, then carefully slide out the baking parchment. Bake the pizza for a further 15 minutes, or until the crust is golden and the cheese melted and bubbling. Remove from the oven and sprinkle with freshly ground black pepper. Eat immediately.

GARLIC MUSHROOM PIZZA

Pizza ai funghi e aglio

½ recipe Basic Pizza Dough (page 12), making just 1 ball of dough

50–75 g/2–3 oz. buffalo mozzarella or cow's milk mozzarella (*fior di latte*)

50 g/½ cup fresh breadcrumbs

30 g/¼ cup freshly grated Parmesan cheese

4 garlic cloves, finely chopped

4 tablespoons chopped fresh parsley

30 g/2 tablespoons butter, melted

about 12 medium chestnut/cremini mushrooms

extra virgin olive oil, to drizzle

sea salt and freshly ground black pepper

a testo, terracotta baking stone or a large, heavy baking sheet

a pizza peel or rimless baking sheet

MAKES 1 MEDIUM-CRUST PIZZA (25–35 CM/10–14 INCHES)

This makes a change from the normal scattering of token sliced mushrooms: here we have fresh mushrooms in all their glory, under a crispy garlicky topping of breadcrumbs and Parmesan. Don't use white mushrooms for this – they often have little or no taste at all. Chestnut/cremini or Portobello mushrooms are ideal.

Put the testo, baking stone or a large, heavy baking sheet on the lower shelf of the oven. Preheat the oven to 220°C (425°F) Gas 7 for at least 30 minutes.

Lightly squeeze any excess moisture out of the mozzarella, then slice or chop into cubes. Mix the breadcrumbs with the Parmesan, garlic and parsley then stir in the melted butter. Lightly fill the cavities of the mushrooms with the breadcrumb mixture.

Uncover the dough, punch out the air and roll or pull into a 25-cm/10-inch circle directly onto baking parchment. Slide this onto the pizza peel or rimless baking sheet. Arrange the mozzarella over the pizza crust leaving a 2.5-cm/1-inch rim around the edge. Arrange the stuffed mushrooms all over, sprinkling any remaining breadcrumbs over the finished pizza. Drizzle with olive oil and season.

Working quickly, open the oven door and slide paper and pizza onto the hot baking stone or baking sheet. If you are brave, try to shoot the pizza into the oven so that it leaves the paper behind – this takes practice!

Bake for 5 minutes, then slide out the baking parchment if possible (this will be quite difficult with the wobbly mushrooms). Bake for a further 15 minutes or until the crust is golden, the cheese melted and the mushrooms tender and bubbling. Remove from the oven and drizzle with olive oil. Eat immediately.

'NDUJA, BROCCOLI, BLACK OLIVE AND EGG PIZZA

Pizza Calabrese

½ recipe Basic Pizza Dough (page 12), or Basic Sourdough Pizza Dough (page 15), making just 1 ball of dough

3–4 tablespoons Pizzaiola Sauce (page 19)

50 g/2 oz. purple sprouting broccoli or other broccoli (see recipe introduction), sliced in half lengthways

100 g/3½ oz. 'nduja (spicy Calabrian sausage)

1 teaspoon dried oregano

5–7 wrinkly black olives, stoned/pitted

1 fresh free-range egg

extra virgin olive oil, to drizzle

sea salt and freshly ground black pepper

a testo, terracotta bakestone or a large, heavy baking sheet

a pizza peel or rimless baking sheet

MAKES 1 MEDIUM-CRUST PIZZA (25–35 CM/10–14 INCHES)

A poem of Calabrian flavours on a pizza! Try tracking down rapini, known for its earthy, slightly bitter taste and beloved by Italian and Spanish cooks. It is not related to broccoli at all but is related to the turnip. In different parts of Italy, it is confusingly known as *cima di rape* ('turnip tops'), *broccoli rabe, friarielli, broccoletti, broccoli friarelli, broccoli di rape, rapi* or *rapini*. (USA broccoli raab, rabe, rab, rape). However if not available, turnip or beetroot/beet tops are a good substitute, then purple sprouting broccoli, tenderstem broccoli and last of all, normal broccoli.

Put the testo, terracotta bakestone or a large, heavy baking sheet on the lower shelf of the oven. Preheat the oven to 220°C (425°F) Gas 7 for at least 30 minutes.

Blanche the broccoli in boiling salted water for 30 seconds, then drain and refresh in cold water.

Uncover the dough, punch out the air and roll or pull into a 25-cm/10-inch circle directly onto non-stick baking parchment. Slide this onto the pizza peel or rimless baking sheet. Spread the pizzaiola sauce over the pizza base, leaving a 1-cm/⅜-inch rim around the edge. Spoon over the 'nduja. Drain the broccoli and scatter over the pizza. Sprinkle with the dried oregano, then the olives, drizzle with olive oil, then season.

Working quickly, open the oven door and slide paper and pizza onto the hot bakestone or baking sheet. If you are brave, try to shoot the pizza into the oven so that it leaves the paper behind – this takes practice!

Bake for 5 minutes, then carefully slide out the baking parchment. Bake the pizza for a further 10 minutes then break the egg into the middle (if using) and bake for 5 minutes, or until the egg is just cooked and the crust is golden. Remove from the oven and drizzle with olive oil. Eat immediately.

QUINOA PIADINE WITH BURRATA, ARTICHOKE AND LEMON AND OLIVE TAPENADE

Piadina di quinoa con burrata, carciofi, limone e crema di olive

125 g/1¼ cup quinoa flour

125 g/1 cup buckwheat or brown rice flour

½ level teaspoon bicarbonate of/ baking soda

25 ml/1¾ tablespoons extra virgin olive oil

approximately 175 ml/¾ cup warm water

250 g/9 oz. burrata cheese, roughly chopped

200 g/7 oz. artichokes preserved in oil (or grilled/broiled artichokes from a deli)

LEMON AND OLIVE TAPENADE:

50 g/2 oz. preserved lemon, skin and flesh finely chopped

50 g/2 oz. stoned/pitted green olives, finely chopped

25 ml/1¾ tablespoons extra virgin olive oil (or chilli/chili oil for a fiery kick), plus extra to drizzle

2 tablespoons chopped fresh basil, plus extra to garnish

sea salt and freshly ground black pepper

a testo, terracotta bakestone or a large, heavy baking sheet

a pizza peel or rimless baking sheet

MAKES 2 THIN PIADINE (25–30 CM/10–12 INCHES)

This gluten-free quinoa dough is very versatile – make one large pizza-size or small snack-size *piadine*. It can even be stamped out into mini bases for cocktail nibbles. It is a great alternative to pizza dough, is more like a crisp tortilla and has a lovely nutty flavour. Quinoa flour is readily available in health food shops.

Sift the flours and bicarbonate of/baking soda into a bowl, make a well in the centre and pour in the olive oil and a pinch of salt to taste. Gradually add the warm water mixing with clean hands until you have a soft dough. Tip out onto a floured surface and knead lightly until smooth. Divide in two, shape into balls, pop into plastic bags and leave to rest for 30 minutes.

Put the testo, terracotta bakestone or a large, heavy baking sheet on the lower shelf of the oven. Preheat the oven to 220°C (425°F) Gas 7 for at least 30 minutes.

To make the lemon and olive tapenade, mix the preserved lemon, olives, olive oil and basil together. Season to taste and set aside.

Remove the dough from the bags, roll out each ball into a 25–30-cm/10–12-inch circle on non-stick baking parchment and slide this onto the pizza peel or rimless baking sheet. Lightly spread the bases with half the tapenade. Scatter the burrata over the bases, leaving a 1-cm/³⁄₈-inch rim around the edge. Arrange the drained artichokes on top, brush with the remaining tapenade, then season.

Working quickly, open the oven door and slide paper and pizza onto the hot bakestone or baking sheet. If you are brave, try to shoot the pizza into the oven so that it leaves the paper behind – this takes practice!

Bake for 5 minutes, then carefully slide out the baking parchment. Bake the *piadine* for a further 8 minutes, or until the crust is golden and crisping. Remove from the oven, scatter with extra basil and drizzle with extra olive oil. Eat immediately.

CARAMELIZED RED ONION PIZZAS WITH CAPERS AND OLIVES

Pizza con cipolle rosse, capperi e olive

1 recipe Basic Pizza Dough (page 12), dividing the dough into 6–8 balls

1 kg/2¼ lb. red onions, finely sliced

freshly squeezed juice of 1 lemon

4 tablespoons olive oil, plus extra to drizzle

2 teaspoons dried oregano

1 mozzarella, drained and thinly sliced

2 tablespoons freshly grated Parmesan cheese

12 anchovy fillets in oil, drained (optional)

15 black olives, stoned/pitted

2 tablespoons capers in salt, washed and drained

sea salt and freshly ground black pepper

2 testi, terracotta baking stones or large, heavy baking sheets

2 rimless baking sheets

MAKES 6–8 PIZZAS DEPENDING ON SIZE

With no hint of tomato sauce, this is a succulent pizza where the onions are cooked until soft and caramelized, before being spread on the pizza on top of the mozzarella. Olives, capers and anchovies add savouriness to the sweet onions. You may leave out the anchovies and add tuna or sardines instead.

Put the testi, baking stones or large, heavy baking sheets on the lower shelves of the oven. Preheat the oven to 220°C (425°F) Gas 7 for at least 30 minutes.

Toss the onions in the lemon juice to coat them thoroughly. Heat the oil in a large, shallow saucepan and add the onions. Cook over a gentle heat for about 10 minutes, stirring occasionally, until they are beginning to colour. Stir in the dried oregano.

Uncover the dough balls, punch out the air and roll or pull each one into a thin circle or oval directly onto separate sheets of baking parchment. Slide these onto 2 rimless baking sheets.

Cover the pizza crusts with the mozzarella leaving a 1-cm/³⁄₈-inch rim around the edge. Top with the onions and sprinkle with the Parmesan. Scatter the anchovy fillets, olives and capers over the top. Drizzle with olive oil, then season, but don't use too much salt as the capers will be salty.

Working quickly, open the oven door and slide paper and pizzas onto the hot baking stones or baking sheets. Bake for 15–20 minutes or until the crust is golden. Remove from the oven and drizzle with olive oil. Eat immediately.

SICILIAN SHRIMP AND TOMATO PIZZA

Pizza ai gamberoni di Sicilia

Using the plumpest raw prawns/shrimp you can find will ensure that they don't toughen up through overcooking. Avoid using pre-cooked prawns/shrimp which will make the end result dry, chewy and unappetizing. If you do have to use the precooked variety, pop them onto the pizza 5 minutes from the end of cooking time.

½ recipe Sicilian Pizza Dough (page 16), making just 1 ball of dough

3–4 tablespoons Pizzaiola Sauce (page 19)

3 garlic cloves, sliced thinly

½ teaspoon dried chilli/hot red pepper flakes

10–12 medium uncooked prawns/shrimp (tails on)

200 g/7 oz. very ripe cherry tomatoes or any other very tasty small tomatoes

a good handful of fresh flat-leaf parsley, roughly chopped

extra virgin olive oil, to drizzle

sea salt and freshly ground black pepper

lemon wedges, to serve

a testo, terracotta baking stone or a large, heavy baking sheet

a pizza peel or rimless baking sheet

MAKES 1 MEDIUM-CRUST PIZZA (25–35 CM/10–14 INCHES)

Put the testo, baking stone or a large, heavy baking sheet on the lower shelf of the oven. Preheat the oven to 220°C (425°F) Gas 7 for at least 30 minutes.

Uncover the dough, punch out the air and roll or pull into a 25-cm/10-inch circle directly onto baking parchment. Slide this onto the pizza peel or rimless baking sheet. Spread the pizzaiola sauce over the pizza crust, leaving a 1-cm/³⁄₈-inch rim around the edge. Scatter with the garlic, dried chilli/hot red pepper flakes, prawns/shrimp and tomatoes. Season.

Working quickly, open the oven door and slide paper and pizza onto the hot baking stone or baking sheet. If you are brave, try to shoot the pizza into the oven so that it leaves the paper behind – this takes practice!

Bake for 5 minutes, then carefully slide out the baking parchment. Bake the pizza for a further 15 minutes, or until the crust is golden and the shrimp are cooked. Remove from the oven, scatter with the parsley and drizzle with olive oil. Eat immediately with the lemon wedges for squeezing over the pizza.

PANCETTA PIZZA

Pizza con pancetta

This is a real favourite of mine. I use very thinly sliced smoked pancetta (the Italian equivalent of bacon, made from salt-cured pork belly). Pancetta comes in many forms: in whole cured slabs (with or without herbs and spices), smoked or unsmoked, or rolled up for slicing thinly, aged or not. The choice is endless and varies from region to region. Outside Italy, you can buy the smoked slab with rind, ready-sliced smoked or rolled unsmoked pancetta. Combined with Fiery Red Pesto, this is incredible!

Put the testo, baking stone or a large, heavy baking sheet on the lower shelf of the oven. Preheat the oven to 220°C (425°F) Gas 7 for at least 30 minutes.

Uncover the dough, punch out the air and roll or pull into a rectangle, about 20 cm/8 inches wide and as long as your oven will take (you can always make 2 shorter ones). Roll the dough directly onto baking parchment.

Slide this onto the pizza peel or rimless baking sheet.

Spread the red pesto over the pizza crust, leaving a 1-cm/³/₈-inch rim around the edge. Lay the strips of pancetta widthways across the pizza – they should be almost the same width as the dough. Season and drizzle with oil.

Working quickly, open the oven door and slide paper and pizza onto the hot baking stone or baking sheet. If you are brave, try to shoot the pizza into the oven so that it leaves the paper behind – this takes practice!

Bake for 5 minutes, then carefully slide out the baking parchment. Bake the pizza for a further 15 minutes, or until the crust is golden and the pancetta crisp. Remove from the oven and drizzle with olive oil. Cut into fingers and eat immediately.

1 recipe Basic Pizza Dough (page 12)

6 tablespoons Fiery Red Pesto (page 23)

24 thin slices pancetta or bacon

extra virgin olive oil, to drizzle

sea salt and freshly ground black pepper

a testo, terracotta baking stone or a large, heavy baking sheet

a pizza peel or rimless baking sheet

MAKES 1 MEDIUM-CRUST PIZZA (APPROXIMATELY 20 X 40 CM/8 X 16 INCHES)

PIZZA WITH ARTICHOKES AND MOZZARELLA

Pizza ai carciofi e scamorza

½ recipe Basic Pizza Dough (page 12), making just 1 ball of dough

100 g/3½ oz. buffalo mozzarella or cow's milk mozzarella (*fior di latte*)

100 g/3½ oz. artichokes preserved in oil or grilled/broiled artichokes from a deli

1–2 garlic cloves, finely chopped

2 tablespoons extra virgin olive oil, plus extra to drizzle

6–8 juicy black olives

2 tablespoons roughly chopped fresh flat-leaf parsley

sea salt and freshly ground black pepper

a testo, terracotta baking stone or a large, heavy baking sheet

a pizza peel or rimless baking sheet

MAKES 1 MEDIUM-CRUST PIZZA, (25–35 CM/10–14 INCHES) **OR 2 SMALL PIZZAS**

Artichokes preserved in oil for antipasti are perfect for pizza-making as the delicious oil they are soaked in means they won't dry out during cooking. I have also made this with smoked mozzarella and it is equally delicious.

Put the testo, baking stone or a large, heavy baking sheet on the lower shelf of the oven. Preheat the oven to 220°C (425°F) Gas 7 for at least 30 minutes.

Lightly squeeze any excess moisture out of the mozzarella, then slice it and leave the slices on paper towels for 5 minutes to absorb any remaining moisture.

Uncover the dough, punch out the air and roll or pull into a 25-cm/10-inch circle or two small circles directly onto baking parchment. Slide this onto the pizza peel or rimless baking sheet. Arrange the mozzarella evenly over the pizza base, leaving a 1-cm/³/₈-inch rim around the edge. Scatter the artichokes and olives over the top, then season and drizzle with olive oil.

Working quickly, open the oven door and slide paper and pizza onto the hot baking stone or baking sheet. If you are brave, try to shoot the pizza into the oven so that it leaves the paper behind – this takes practice!

Bake for 5 minutes, then carefully slide out the baking parchment. Bake the pizza for a further 15 minutes, or until the crust is golden and the cheese melted and bubbling. Remove from the oven and sprinkle the parsley and freshly ground black pepper over the top. Eat immediately.

PIZZA PICCANTE

½ recipe Sicilian Pizza Dough
(page 16), making just 1 ball of dough

4 tablespoons Pizzaiola Sauce
(page 19)

50 g/2 oz. buffalo mozzarella or
cow's milk mozzarella (*fior di latte*)

3 large garlic cloves, thinly sliced

50 g/2 oz. *provolone piccante*,
thinly sliced

2 fat red chillies/chiles (or more),
thinly sliced

extra virgin olive oil, to drizzle

chilli/chili oil, to drizzle

sea salt and freshly ground
black pepper

*a testo, terracotta baking stone
or a large, heavy baking sheet*

a pizza peel or rimless baking sheet

MAKES 1 MEDIUM-CRUST
PIZZA (25–35 CM/10–14 INCHES)

This contains all the heat of southern Italy. *Provolone piccante*, originally from Campania, is a sharp, aged cow's cheese often found in a globe shape and usually covered in a waxed rind. It makes a delicious sandwich with fresh tomato, dried oregano and a drizzle of olive oil.

Put the testo, baking stone or a large, heavy baking sheet on the lower shelf of the oven. Preheat the oven to 220°C (425°F) Gas 7 for at least 30 minutes.

Lightly squeeze any excess moisture out of the mozzarella, then slice it and leave the slices on paper towels for 5 minutes to absorb any remaining moisture.

Uncover the dough, punch out the air and roll or pull into a 25-cm/ 10-inch circle directly onto baking parchment. Slide this onto the pizza peel or rimless baking sheet. Spread the pizzaiola sauce over the pizza crust, leaving a 1-cm/³⁄₈-inch rim around the edge. Scatter the garlic over the top. Arrange the provolone and mozzarella on top and scatter with the chillies/chiles. Season well with plenty of ground black pepper and drizzle with olive oil.

Working quickly, open the oven door and slide paper and pizza onto the hot baking stone or baking sheet. If you are brave, try to shoot the pizza into the oven so that it leaves the paper behind – this takes practice!

Bake for 5 minutes, then carefully slide out the baking parchment. Bake the pizza for a further 15 minutes, or until the crust is golden and the cheese melted and bubbling. Remove from the oven and drizzle with the chilli/chili oil. Eat immediately.

Little Tuscan Pizzas

Schiacciate Toscana

1 recipe Basic Pizza Dough (page 12)

CHOOSE FROM THE FOLLOWING TOPPINGS (THINLY SLICE ANY VEGETABLES AND MOZZARELLA):

salami, red onion and capers

aubergine/eggplant, red onions, mozzarella and sage

potato, mozzarella, anchovy, olive sage or rosemary

courgette/zucchini, mozzarella, anchovy and basil

mozzarella, tomato and rocket/arugula

extra virgin olive oil, to drizzle

sea salt and freshly ground black pepper

2 heavy baking sheets

MAKES 6 SMALL, THIN PIZZAS

Schiacciate (skee-a-chah-tay) in Tuscany are individual thin, crispy pizzas with the simplest of toppings. Forget Neapolitan pizzas – the dough is rolled out to almost baking-parchment thinness, laid on an oiled tray, then topped with cheese, vegetables and prosciutto, all of which are cut wafer-thin so that they will cook quickly. Mozzarella is often used as the base instead of tomato sauce and sliced fresh tomatoes or halved cherry tomatoes are scattered on top of the cheese. Fresh herbs or a handful of peppery rocket/arugula are often added when the pizza comes sizzling out of the oven.

Place 2 heavy baking sheets in the oven. Preheat the oven to 220°C (425°F) Gas 7 for at least 30 minutes.

Uncover the dough, punch out the air and divide into 6. Shape each piece into a smooth ball and roll into a very thin circle. Put the disks on a couple of baking sheets lined with baking parchment. Arrange a few slices of mozzarella on top (if using). Toss the chosen sliced vegetables in a little olive oil and arrange sparingly on top of the pizza crusts along with any other toppings.

Working quickly, open the oven door and slide paper and pizzas onto the hot baking sheets. Bake the pizzas for 15–20 minutes, or until the crust is golden and crisp. Remove from the oven, scatter with any herbs or leaves, drizzle with olive oil and serve immediately.

PEAR, PECORINO AND TALEGGIO PIZZA WITH HONEY AND SAGE

Pizza con pere, pecorino, Taleggio, salvia e miele

½ recipe Basic Pizza Dough (page 12), making just 1 ball of dough

2 tablespoons extra virgin olive oil, plus extra to drizzle

125 g/4 oz. Taleggio (rind removed), cubed

1 very ripe pear, cored and thinly sliced

12–15 small sage leaves

50 g/½ cup freshly grated pecorino cheese

1 tablespoon honey (acacia or orange blossom, if possible)

sea salt and freshly ground black pepper

a testo, terracotta baking stone or a large, heavy baking sheet

a pizza peel or rimless baking sheet

MAKES 1 MEDIUM-CRUST PIZZA (25–35 CM/10–14 INCHES)

This is a sort of new-wave pizza and very popular in Italian city pizzerias. Soft, buttery Taleggio, made in the valleys and mountains of Lombardy and the Valtellina, melts and runs very quickly, so make sure it's not near the edge of the pizza. Ripe, juicy pear is the perfect foil for this cheese and don't leave out the sage – it's integral to the flavour.

Put the testo, baking stone or a large, heavy baking sheet on the lower shelf of the oven. Preheat the oven to 220°C (425°F) Gas 7 for at least 30 minutes.

Uncover the dough, punch out the air and roll or pull into a 25-cm/10-inch circle directly onto baking parchment. Slide this onto the pizza peel or rimless baking sheet. Rub the pizza crust with the olive oil and scatter over the Taleggio. Arrange the pear over this, then the sage and pecorino. Drizzle with the honey, then season and drizzle with a little more olive oil.

Working quickly, open the oven door and slide paper and pizza onto the hot baking stone or baking sheet. If you are brave, try to shoot the pizza into the oven so that it leaves the paper behind – this takes practice!

Bake for 5 minutes, then carefully slide out the baking parchment. Bake the pizza for a further 15 minutes, or until the crust is golden and the cheese melted and bubbling. Sprinkle with freshly ground black pepper and eat immediately.

Sprout, Burrata and Pancetta Pizza with Garlic and Lemon Oil

Pizza con burrata, cavoletti di Bruxelles, pancetta e con olio all'aglio e limone

½ recipe either Basic Pizza Dough (page 12) or Basic Sourdough Pizza Dough (page 15), making just 1 ball of dough

GARLIC AND LEMON OIL:

3 tablespoons extra virgin olive oil

2 garlic cloves, sliced

finely grated zest of ½ lemon

150 g/5½ oz. burrata cheese (or fresh buffalo mozzarella)

10 Brussels sprouts, finely shredded

freshly grated nutmeg, to taste

5 thin slices pancetta

sea salt and freshly ground black pepper

a testo, terracotta bakestone or a large, heavy baking sheet

a pizza peel or rimless baking sheet

MAKES 1 THIN-CRUST PIZZA (35 CM/14 INCHES)

Originally from Puglia, burrata has a thin-spun casing of spun mozzarella and a soft, buttery centre of fresh cream and unspun mozzarella curds. This results in a wickedly creamy cheese with a hint of acidic sweetness. It is usually eaten on its own with fresh ripe tomatoes and olive oil, but here it is combined with sweet sprouts and pancetta for total indulgence.

Put the testo, terracotta bakestone or a large, heavy baking sheet on the lower shelf of the oven. Preheat the oven to 220°C (425°F) Gas 7 for at least 30 minutes.

To make the garlic and lemon oil, put the olive oil, sliced garlic, lemon zest, with salt and pepper to taste into a very small pan and heat gently without boiling for 5 minutes (alternatively warm in microwave). Set aside to infuse while the oven heats up.

Uncover the dough, punch out the air and roll or pull into a 35-cm/14-inch circle directly onto non-stick baking parchment. Slide this onto the pizza peel or rimless baking sheet. Brush the dough all over with the garlic and lemon oil, reserving some for drizzling once cooked. Scatter the sliced burrata over the pizza base, leaving a 1-cm/³/₈-inch rim around the edge. Now top with the shredded sprouts and grate a little nutmeg over the top. Rip up the pancetta and dot this over the surface then season.

Working quickly, open the oven door and slide paper and pizza onto the hot bakestone or baking sheet. If you are brave, try to shoot the pizza into the oven so that it leaves the paper behind – this takes practice!

Bake for 5 minutes, then carefully slide out the baking parchment. Bake the pizza for a further 8–10 minutes, or until the crust is golden, the cheese bubbling and the pancetta crisped. Remove from the oven and drizzle with the remaining garlic and lemon oil. Eat immediately.

PALERMO PIZZA

Sfinciune

2 recipes Sicilian Pizza Dough
(page 16), making the changes
stated in this recipe

7 tablespoons olive oil, plus extra
to drizzle

1 large onion, sliced

3 large ripe tomatoes, chopped

1 teaspoon dried oregano,
plus extra to taste

8 anchovy fillets in oil,
drained and chopped

75 g/1 cup dried breadcrumbs

75 g/2½ oz. *caciocavallo*
(or Emmental), cubed

sea salt and freshly ground
black pepper

a rectangular baking pan,
35 x 25 x 3 cm/14 x 10 x 1¼ inches,
oiled

a testo, terracotta baking stone
or a large, heavy baking sheet

MAKES 1 THICK PIZZA
(25 X 35 CM/14 X 10 INCHES)

You will see mounds of this thick pizza on food stalls all over Palermo. It is the ultimate snack on the run and is perfect for picnics and lunchboxes. It may seem strange, but in Sicily, breadcrumbs are sprinkled over pasta and even on top of pizza. Very often this dough is made in two stages: a loose batter is made and left to rise, then the remaining ingredients are kneaded in and left to rise again, but my method reduces the time. Make sure you use good olive oil here.

When you make the pizza dough, replace the lemon juice with olive oil. Rise once, then punch down the air, knead lightly and roll or pull into a rectangle that will fit into the prepared baking pan. Cover the pan lightly with clingfilm/plastic wrap or a damp kitchen towel and leave in a warm place to rise until it has reached the top of the pan (about 30 minutes).

While the dough is rising, put the testo, baking stone or a large, heavy baking sheet on the lower shelf of the oven. Preheat the oven to 220°C (425°F) Gas 7 for at least 30 minutes.

To make the sauce, heat 4 tablespoons of the olive oil in a saucepan and add the onion. Cook until soft but not coloured, then add the tomatoes, dried oregano and anchovy fillets. Cook for 5 minutes until the anchovies dissolve and the tomatoes collapse. Season to taste.

Heat the remaining olive oil in a frying pan/skillet and fry the breadcrumbs until golden and crisp.

When the dough has risen, uncover and dimple the top lightly with your fingers as if you were making focaccia, but don't make too many holes. Spread with half of the sauce and bake for 25 minutes.

Remove from the oven, spread the remaining sauce over the top, scatter over the breadcrumbs and extra oregano and drizzle with olive oil. Finish by scattering the caciocavallo over everything, then bake for another 5 minutes until the top is golden. Serve warm or cold, cut into squares.

CRISPY OLIVE 'PIZZA'

Schiacciata croccante con olive

any leftover Basic Pizza Dough
(page 12)

a splash of white wine

a handful of green olives, stoned/pitted
and roughly chopped

coarse sea salt

extra virgin olive oil or Black Olive
and Tomato Relish (page 23), to serve

a testo, terracotta baking stone
or a large, heavy baking sheet

a large rimless baking sheet

Schiacciata is a dialect word meaning 'flattened,' so pizza is sometimes known as *schiacciata* – a flattened bread dough. After making pizza one day, I had some dough left over and devised this 'pizza' using leftover olives. There is no olive oil needed here, but you can have some really good oil in a little pot ready for dipping the hot pizzas into. Alternatively, you could pile on some Black Olive and Tomato Relish (page 23) as the schiacciate come out of the oven.

Put the testo, terracotta bakestone or a large, heavy baking sheet on the lower shelf of the oven. Preheat the oven to 220°C (425°F) Gas 7 for at least 30 minutes.

Using a rolling pin, roll the dough out as thinly as you can, directly onto the baking sheet. Brush the dough with a little white wine, scatter with the olives and sprinkle with salt. Lightly press the olives and salt into the dough. Using a pizza wheel, score the dough in lozenge shapes directly on the baking sheet.

Bake for 5–10 minutes until the pizzas are puffed and pale golden. Remove from the oven and break up into the pre-cut lozenges. Serve warm with olive oil or Black Olive and Tomato Relish.

POTATO PIZZA

Pizza di patate

750 g/1¾ lb. floury baking potatoes (King Edwards, Golden Wonder, Red Rooster), unpeeled

2 tablespoons olive oil, plus extra to drizzle

6–8 cherry or baby plum tomatoes, halved

50 g/½ cup black wrinkly olives

25 g/2 tablespoons salted capers, rinsed

3 salted anchovies, rinsed

1 small red onion, sliced into thin rings and tossed in olive oil

1 teaspoon dried oregano

sea salt and freshly ground black pepper

a pizza pan, 23 cm/9 inches, oiled

MAKES 1 PIZZA
(23 CM/9 INCHES)

Although not crispy like a pizza, this is a wonderful alternative for those who love mashed potatoes or who are wheat-intolerant and it is popular in southern Italian homes. If you are not keen on anchovies, try using canned tuna – you can really try any pizza topping you like, even mozzarella. Have some pizzaiola sauce to serve on the side, along with grilled sausages for any meat-eaters. Other recipes for potato pizza incorporate mashed potatoes in normal pizza dough, which is delicious, but a little heavy and obviously not wheat-free!

Preheat the oven to 200°C (400°F) Gas 6.

Boil the potatoes in plenty of salted water until tender. Drain well and carefully peel off the skins. Mash the potatoes or push them through a potato ricer, then let cool for 5 minutes. Beat in the olive oil and season to taste. Spoon into the prepared pizza pan and smooth out the surface.

Top with the tomatoes, olives, capers, anchovies and onion rings.

Sprinkle with the dried oregano and drizzle with olive oil. Bake in the oven for 20 minutes until sizzling. Serve hot or cold.

WHEAT-FREE PIZZA WITH ROASTED VEGETABLES

Pizza senza grano con verdure arrosto

½ aubergine/eggplant, cubed

1 small red (bell) pepper, seeded and cut into strips

1 small courgette/zucchini, sliced

2 garlic cloves, sliced

6 tablespoons olive oil, plus extra to drizzle

3 tablespoons each milk and water, mixed together and warmed

¾ teaspoon freshly squeezed lemon juice

1 egg

½ teaspoon salt

225 g/1¾ cups gluten-free white bread flour

1 teaspoon fast-action dried yeast

75 g/2½ oz. mozzarella, drained and cubed (optional)

sea salt and freshly ground black pepper

a shallow pizza pan, 23 cm/9 inches, oiled

MAKES 1 PIZZA (23 CM/9 INCHES)

This wheat-free pizza is very good, but don't expect a pizza-like dough. It starts life as a batter and when baked, becomes chewy and sponge-like on the inside, with a crisp crust. I suggest using a gluten-free flour that is a mix of rice, potato and tapioca flours blended with xanthan gum. I developed this recipe for those who can't eat wheat but still crave that unique pizza experience. You could also try mixing in other gluten-free flours, such as chickpea or buckwheat.

Preheat the oven to 200°C (400°F) Gas 6.

Toss the aubergine/eggplant, red (bell) pepper, courgette/zucchini and garlic in 4 tablespoons of the olive oil and roast in a roasting pan in the oven for 15–20 minutes, or until they are beginning to soften.

While the vegetables are roasting, make the batter. Whisk the warm (not hot) milk and water, the lemon juice, remaining olive oil, egg and salt together. Beat in the flour and yeast and mix until well combined. Pour into the prepared pizza pan, cover and let rise in a warm place for about 20 minutes or until puffy.

Bake the pizza crust in the oven for 10 minutes to set the dough, then quickly remove from the oven and scatter with the roasted vegetables and mozzarella (if using). Season well, drizzle with olive oil and return to the oven for a further 10 minutes until the vegetables are sizzling and the pizza has slightly shrunk from the edges. Cut into wedges and serve hot.

FLATBREADS FROM EMILIA ROMAGNA

Piadine

500 g/4¼ cups Italian '0' or '00' flour, or unbleached plain/all-purpose flour

1 teaspoon baking powder

a pinch of fine sea salt

4 tablespoons good olive oil, melted unsalted butter or pure lard (*strutto*)

200 ml/¾ cup hand-hot water

a testo, iron griddle or heavy-based frying pan/skillet

MAKES ABOUT 8 FLATBREADS

A *piadina* ('little plate') is traditionally cooked on a testo (a thick, flat piece of terracotta, see page 9). As these are difficult to buy outside Italy, I use unglazed terracotta plant-pot saucers with great success. Never oil a testo – it must be clean and dry. Heat it gently over a low heat, gradually increasing the heat to medium. Alternatively, use an iron griddle or a heavy-based frying pan/skillet, but make sure it is hot before using it. Keep the *piadine* warm and soft inside a folded napkin in a basket until they are ready to serve. Serve them warm, folded over, with thinly sliced prosciutto crudo or salami piled inside.

Sift the flour, baking powder and salt into a large bowl. Make a well in the centre and pour in the oil and the hand-hot water to make a soft dough. Add more water if the dough looks dry. Knead for a couple of minutes or until smooth, wrap in clingfilm/plastic wrap and let rest at room temperature for 30 minutes.

Divide the dough into 8, keeping the pieces covered under an upturned bowl. Roll each into a thin 20-cm/8-inch disk. Stack these up with baking parchment or clingfilm/plastic wrap between each and cover with clingfilm/plastic wrap or a damp kitchen towel.

Heat the testo on the stovetop until medium hot. Slide a disk onto the hot testo and cook for 30–40 seconds until brown spots appear on the underside. Flip it over and cook for a further 30 seconds or until both sides are dry-looking and covered with brown spots or blisters (like a tortilla or Indian chappati). Avoid cooking them for too long as they will end up being dry and tough.

Keep the cooked flatbreads warm inside a folded napkin or loosely wrapped in foil in a warm oven while cooking the remainder. They are best served warm.

CHICKPEA AND ROSEMARY FLATBREAD

Farinata

4 tablespoons extra virgin olive oil

200 g/1⅔ cups Italian chickpea flour or gram flour

1 teaspoon sea salt, plus extra to sprinkle

4 sprigs of fresh rosemary, leaves stripped off

freshly ground black pepper

a pizza pan, 28 cm/11 inches, preferably non-stick

MAKES 1 FLATBREAD
(28 CM/11 INCHES)

Farinata is a Ligurian specialty and should be made with very good olive oil. It is traditionally baked in a large, shallow copper pan, but a wide metal pizza pan will do. It is often cut into lozenge shapes and eaten as a snack. I like to make it into a type of pizza for those who can't eat wheat: I cook it for 10 minutes or until just set, strew prawns/shrimp, tomatoes and diced pancetta on top, then cook until firm and golden. The batter itself can be flavoured with chopped rosemary, dried chilli/hot red pepper flakes or black pepper. If you can't find Italian chickpea flour, use Indian gram flour (available in Asian food stores) although the colour will be paler.

Put 500 ml/2 cups cold water in a bowl with 1 tablespoon of the olive oil. Gradually beat in the chickpea flour and salt until smooth and creamy. Cover and let stand for at least 30 minutes, or overnight in the refrigerator if possible.

Preheat the oven to 220°C (425°F) Gas 7 or hotter, if possible.

Oil the pizza pan with the remaining olive oil. It must be well oiled to give the right flavour and ensure a crisp edge.

Stir the batter and pour into the prepared pizza pan. Sprinkle the rosemary on top and bake for about 20 minutes or until set and golden. Serve warm, cut into slices or lozenge shapes and sprinkled with salt and pepper.

KIMCHI AND MEATBALL PIZZA WITH SOY–LIME GLAZE

Pizza con kimchi e polpettine glassate con salsa di soia e limetta

1 recipe Basic Pizza Dough (page 12)

200 g/7 oz. smoked firm tofu, grated

KIMCHI SALAD:

1 small cucumber

1 large carrot

3 spring onions/scallions

25 g/1 oz. grated fresh ginger

2 garlic cloves, thinly sliced

2 teaspoons caster/granulated sugar

1–2 teaspoons fish sauce

1–2 teaspoons soy sauce

2 teaspoons rice vinegar

6–8 sprigs fresh coriander/cilantro

MEATBALLS:

2 tablespoons milk

1 small egg, lightly beaten

4 tablespoons fine dried breadcrumbs

350 g/12 oz. minced/ground pork

1 small can water chestnuts, drained and finely chopped

3 tablespoons chopped fresh coriander/cilantro

2 teaspoons soy sauce

1 teaspoon sesame oil

SOY–LIME GLAZE:

4 tablespoons soy sauce

2 teaspoons sesame oil

4 tablespoons fresh lime juice

2 tablespoons soft brown sugar

2 testi, terracotta bakestone or large, heavy baking sheets

2 rimless baking sheets

MAKES 2 THIN-CRUST PIZZAS
(35 CM/14 INCHES)

An Asian-inspired version of a meatball pizza. The cooked pizza drizzled with sweet and savoury soy–lime glaze is served with a tangle of hot and sour crunchy kimchi salad. There are a lot of ingredients but it's worth it for a special treat!

Make the kimchi salad the day before if possible. Using a potato peeler, shave long strips from the cucumber avoiding the wet seeds. Do the same with the carrot and shred the spring onions/scallions. Mix the ginger, garlic, sugar, fish sauce, soy sauce and rice vinegar together in the bottom of a medium bowl. Throw in the vegetables and toss well to coat. Cover and refrigerate for as long as possible.

Put the testi, terracotta bakestones or large, heavy baking sheets on the lower shelves of the oven. Preheat the oven to 220°C (425°F) Gas 7 for at least 30 minutes.

Meanwhile, to make the meatballs, mix the milk with the egg and breadcrumbs and stir until absorbed. Add the pork, water chestnuts, chopped coriander/cilantro, soy sauce, sesame oil and mix with your hands until well-combined. Take scant tablespoonfuls of the mix and roll each one into a small ball.

For the soy–lime glaze, stir together the soy sauce, sesame oil, lime juice and sugar with 4 tablespoons of water in a small saucepan and boil for 2–3 minutes until slightly thickened. Set aside.

Uncover the dough, punch out the air and roll or pull into two 35-cm/14-inch circles directly onto non-stick baking parchment. Slide these onto the rimless baking sheets. Scatter the tofu over the pizza bases, leaving a 1-cm/³/₈-inch rim around the edge. Arrange the meatballs on top, then working quickly, open the oven door and slide paper and pizzas onto the hot bakestones or baking sheets. If you are brave, try to shoot the pizzas into the oven so that it leaves the paper behind – this takes practice!

Bake for 5 minutes, then carefully slide out the baking parchment. Bake the pizzas for a further 10–15 minutes, or until the crust is golden and the meatballs cooked. Remove from the oven, drizzle with the glaze then divide the kimchi between the two pizzas, piling high. Finish with the coriander/cilantro sprigs and eat immediately.

CALZONES AND PIZZA PIES

1 recipe Basic Pizza Dough
(page 12), up to the first rising

plain/all-purpose flour, for dusting

2 aubergines/eggplants, cubed

12 whole garlic cloves, peeled

4 tablespoons extra virgin olive oil,
plus extra to glaze

200 g/7 oz. buffalo mozzarella or
cow's milk mozzarella (*fior di latte*)

5 ripe tomatoes, cubed

3 tablespoons chopped fresh basil

4 tablespoons freshly grated
Parmesan cheese

sea salt and freshly ground
black pepper

2 large, heavy baking sheets

2 rimless baking sheets

MAKES 4 CALZONES
(20 CM/8 INCHES)

CALZONE ALLA PARMIGIANA

This is a good calzone to make for more than two people. The filling ingredients can be chopped as finely or roughly as you like, but the aubergine/eggplant must be cooked through before it goes into the dough. I sometimes add a couple of tablespoons of Pizzaiola Sauce to the mixture to make it extra tomatoey.

Put the large, heavy baking sheets into the oven. Preheat the oven to 200°C (400°F) Gas 6 for at least 30 minutes.

Uncover the dough, punch out the air and divide into 4 balls. Dredge with flour and let rise on floured baking parchment for 20 minutes, until soft and puffy.

Meanwhile, toss the aubergine/eggplant and garlic cloves with the olive oil in a roasting pan and roast for 20 minutes.

Lightly squeeze any excess moisture out of the mozzarella then cut it into cubes. Remove the roasting pan from the oven and let cool for 10 minutes before stirring in the tomatoes, mozzarella and basil. Season to taste.

Roll or pull the risen balls of dough into 20-cm/8-inch circles directly onto 2 sheets of baking parchment. Slide these onto 2 rimless baking sheets. Spread a quarter of the vegetable mixture on one half of each calzone, leaving just over 1 cm/³/₈ inch around the edge for sealing. Season well. Fold the uncovered half of the dough over the filling. Pinch and twist the edges firmly together so that the filling doesn't escape during cooking. Brush with olive oil and sprinkle with Parmesan.

Working quickly, open the oven door and slide paper and calzones onto the hot baking sheets. Bake for 30 minutes, swapping the baking sheets around halfway or until the crust is puffed up and golden. Remove from the oven and let stand for 2–3 minutes before serving (this will allow the filling to cool slightly). Serve hot or warm.

POTATO AND MOZZARELLA CALZONE

Calzone di patate e mozzarella

½ recipe Basic Pizza Dough
(page 12), making just 1 ball of dough

50–75 g/2–3 oz. buffalo mozzarella
or cow's milk mozzarella (*fior di latte*)

200 g/7 oz. potatoes, peeled and
very thinly sliced

2 tablespoons extra virgin olive oil,
plus extra to glaze

1 garlic clove, finely chopped

1 tablespoon chopped fresh rosemary

sea salt and freshly ground
black pepper

*a testo, terracotta baking stone
or a large, heavy baking sheet*

a pizza peel or rimless baking sheet

MAKES 1 CALZONE
(25–35 CM/10–14 INCHES)

In Naples, this is known as 'filled pizza' or *pizza ripieno*, but the word 'calzone' literally means 'trouser leg' as it was thought the shape was reminiscent of the traditional everyday dress of the street – a sort of tapered pantaloon.

Put the testo, baking stone or a large, heavy baking sheet on the lower shelf of the oven. Preheat the oven to 220°C (425°F) Gas 7 for at least 30 minutes.

Lightly squeeze any excess moisture out of the mozzarella then cut it into cubes. Toss the sliced potato with the olive oil, garlic and rosemary, then add the mozzarella.

Uncover the dough, punch out the air and roll or pull into a 25-cm/10-inch circle directly onto baking parchment. Slide this onto the pizza peel or rimless baking sheet. Spread one half of the calzone with the potato mixture, leaving just over 1 cm/³⁄₈ inch around the edge for sealing. Season well. Fold the uncovered half of the dough over the filling. Pinch and twist the edges firmly together so that the filling doesn't escape during cooking.

Working quickly, open the oven door and slide paper and calzone onto the hot baking stone or baking sheet. If you are brave, try to shoot the calzone into the oven so that it leaves the paper behind – this takes practice!

Bake for 10 minutes, then carefully slide out the baking parchment.

Bake for a further 25–30 minutes or until the crust is puffed up and golden. Remove from the oven and brush with a little olive oil. Let stand for 2–3 minutes before serving (this will allow the filling to cool slightly). Serve hot or warm.

PULLED PORK, SWEET POTATO, ROASTED CORN AND PICCALILLI CALZONE

Calzone ripieno di sfilacci di maiale al forno, patate Americane, granturco arrosto e salsa piccalilli

½ recipe Basic Pizza Dough (page 12), up to the first rising

2 fresh corn cobs/ears, husks removed

2 large sweet potatoes, peeled and diced

300 g/10½ oz. pre-cooked pulled pork

1 tablespoon chopped fresh thyme

3–4 tablespoons good-quality piccalilli, plus extra to serve

extra virgin olive oil, to glaze

sea salt and freshly ground black pepper

2 large, heavy baking sheets

2 rimless baking sheets

MAKES 2 CALZONES
(20 CM/8 INCHES)

A great way to use up any extra pulled pork leftovers and turn them into a real treat. Ready-cooked pulled pork is available from larger supermarkets if there are no leftovers! There's no getting away from this, it is real food for the soul!

Put the heavy baking sheets into the oven. Preheat the oven to 200°C (400°F) Gas 6 for at least 30 minutes. Put the corn cobs/ears in a baking pan and roast in the oven while it is heating. Cook until the corn starts to char a little then remove and cool.

Uncover the dough, punch out the air and divide into 2 balls. Dredge with flour and leave to rise on floured baking parchment for about 20 minutes, until soft and puffy.

Meanwhile, mix the diced sweet potato with the pulled pork, thyme and piccalilli. Cut the kernels from the corn cobs/ears and stir into the mixture. Season to taste.

Roll or pull the risen balls of dough into 20-cm/8-inch circles directly onto 2 sheets of non-stick baking parchment. Slide these onto the rimless baking sheets.

Spoon half the pork mixture on one half of each calzone, leaving just over 1 cm/³⁄₈ inch around the edge for sealing. Season well. Fold the uncovered half of the dough over the filling. Pinch and twist the edges firmly together so that the filling doesn't escape during cooking. Working quickly, open the oven door and slide paper and calzones onto the hot baking sheets. Bake for 30 minutes or until the crust is puffed up and golden.

Remove from the oven and leave to stand for 2–3 minutes before serving (this will allow the filling to cool slightly). Serve hot or warm with extra piccalilli on the side.

EGG AND SPINACH PIZZA PIES

Torte al spinaci, ricotta e uove

These little pies could be made into a traditional calzone by breaking a whole egg into the filling, but for a picnic or a special occasion, they look great cooked in muffin top pans.

1 recipe Basic Pizza Dough (page 12) or Sicilian Pizza Dough (page 16)

2 tablespoons extra virgin olive oil, plus extra to glaze

1 small onion, finely chopped

250 g/9 oz. fresh spinach, washed

250 g/9 oz. ricotta

4 tablespoons freshly grated Parmesan cheese

75 g/2½ cups rocket/arugula, finely chopped

1 teaspoon chopped fresh tarragon

8 eggs

sea salt and freshly ground black pepper

freshly grated nutmeg

a testo, terracotta baking stone or a large, heavy baking sheet

two 4-hole muffin pans

MAKES 8 PIZZA PIES

Place the testo, baking stone or a large, heavy baking sheet on the lower shelf of the oven. Preheat the oven to 220°C (425°F) Gas 7 for at least 30 minutes.

Heat the olive oil in a frying pan/skillet, add the onion and fry for 5 minutes until golden. Let cool. Steam the spinach until just wilted, refresh in cold water, then squeeze out as much moisture as possible and roughly chop. Beat the spinach and onions into the ricotta with the Parmesan, rocket/arugula and tarragon. Season well with salt, pepper and nutmeg.

Uncover the dough, punch out the air, then tip out onto a floured surface. Roll or pull to a thin disk. Cut out 8 circles roughly 16 cm/6 inches in diameter. Use these to line each muffin cup. Fill each pie with some of the ricotta mixture. Make a small indent in each filling. Break the eggs one at a time, separating the yolks from the whites. Slip a yolk and a little white into the indent of each pie. Season. Roll the dough scraps into long, thin ropes and cut into 16 lengths. Use these to make a cross on top of each pie, sealing the edges with a little water. Brush lightly with olive oil.

Bake in the oven for 10 minutes until the egg is just set and the dough cooked. Eat hot from the oven.

STROMBOLI

1 recipe Basic Pizza Dough (page 12) or Sicilian Pizza Dough (page 16)

8 tablespoons Fiery Red Pesto (page 23)

4 large red (bell) peppers

4 tablespoons olive oil

125 g/4 oz. black olives, stoned/pitted and chopped

a large baking sheet, lined with baking parchment

MAKES 4 STROMBOLI

I have never quite worked out why these little filled and rolled pizzas are called *stromboli*. Stromboli is a live volcano and one of the Aeolian islands off the coast of northern Sicily. Maybe it describes the eruption of flavours and filling when the pizzas are cut open, or the black and red colours of the filling. These are better eaten at room temperature and are perfect for picnics and packed lunches. Meat-eaters can cover the red (bell) pepper with slices of cooked ham before rolling up.

Preheat the oven to 200°C (400°F) Gas 6.

Rub the (bell) peppers with the olive oil and roast in the oven for 25–30 minutes until blackened on the outside. Peel the peppers, pull them apart and remove the seeds and stalks. Let cool.

Meanwhile, uncover the dough, punch out the air and knead half of the olives into it. Divide the dough into 4. Roll each piece into a rectangle about 17 x 24 cm/7 x 10 inches. Spread pesto over each one, sprinkle the remaining chopped olives over the top and cover with the peppers, leaving a 1-cm/³/₈-inch rim around the edges of the dough. Roll up from the shorter side. Make sure the seam is underneath the pizza. Pinch the open ends to seal and tuck them under. Squash the rolled pizzas slightly – they should now look a little like French pains au chocolat. Arrange them well apart on the prepared baking sheet, cover with lightly oiled clingfilm/plastic wrap and let rise for 20 minutes.

Remove the clingfilm/plastic wrap and bake the stromboli for 25–30 minutes until risen and golden. Leave to cool for 5 minutes before cutting open and serving, or let cool completely.

Rustic Country Pie

Torta rustica

1 recipe Basic Pizza Dough (page 12)

5 eggs, separated

300 g/10 oz. ricotta, sieved/strained

100 g/3½ oz. cow's milk mozzarella (*fior di latte*), diced

100 g/3½ oz. smoked mozzarella, diced

55 g/2 oz. Speck ham, chopped

55 g/2 oz. salami, chopped

4 tablespoons freshly grated Parmesan cheese

10 cherry tomatoes, halved

sea salt and freshly ground black pepper

a pizza pan or springform cake pan, 25 cm/10 inches and 4 cm/1¾ inches deep, lightly oiled

**MAKES 1 PIE
(25 CM/10 INCHES)**

At one time, this pie was made with sweet pastry but nowadays it is made with pizza dough. You can use any filling you like, but ricotta and pockets of melting mozzarella are essential. It is very rich and filling and equally good eaten at room temperature.

Place a baking sheet in the middle of the oven. Preheat the oven to 180°C (350°F) Gas 4.

Beat 4 of the egg yolks together, then beat into the ricotta with plenty of salt and pepper. Whisk all the egg whites until stiff and fold into the ricotta mixture. Now fold in both types of mozzarella, the Speck and salami and finally the Parmesan.

Uncover the dough, punch out the air and roll or pull two-thirds of it into a 35-cm/14-inch circle. Use this to line the pizza pan, draping the extra dough over the edge. Spoon in the filling and smooth out the surface. Roll out the remaining dough thinly on a floured surface. Cut it into narrow strips and use them to make a lattice over the top of the pie. Secure the ends to the edge of the pastry with a little water. Trim around the edge with a sharp knife. Place a halved cherry tomato in each square of the lattice and season again. Beat the remaining egg yolk with a pinch of salt and brush the edges of the pie with it.

Bake in the oven for 40–45 minutes until golden. Remove from the oven and let stand for 10 minutes before serving.

Aubergine/ Eggplant and tuna double-crust pizza

Scacciata

This magnificent double-crust pie is filled with Sicilian bounty – aubergines/eggplants, tomatoes, tuna and basil. The breadcrumbs between the layers soak up the juices and keep the filling firm but moist. Out of season, canned tuna in oil works very well.

1 recipe Sicilian Pizza Dough (page 16)

4 tablespoons Classic Pesto Genovese (page 20)

4 tablespoons extra virgin olive oil, plus extra to glaze

2 aubergines/eggplants, thinly sliced

55 g/⅔ cup dried breadcrumbs

55 g/½ cup freshly grated pecorino cheese

two 150-g/5-oz. fresh tuna steaks, sliced horizontally

4 tomatoes, thinly sliced

sea salt and freshly ground black pepper

a testo, terracotta baking stone or a large, heavy baking sheet

a pizza pan or springform cake pan, 25 cm/10 inches and 4 cm/1¾ inches deep, lightly oiled

MAKES 1 PIE
(25 CM/10 INCHES)

Put the testo, baking stone or a large, heavy baking sheet on the lower shelf of the oven. Preheat the oven to 220°C (425°F) Gas 7 for at least 30 minutes.

Heat the olive oil in a frying pan/skillet and fry the aubergines/eggplants until golden brown.

Drain on paper towels. Mix the breadcrumbs with the pecorino.

Uncover the dough, punch out the air and roll or pull two-thirds of it into a 35-cm/14-inch circle. Use this to line the pizza pan, draping the extra dough over the edge. Arrange the aubergine/eggplant slices over the crust and sprinkle with a quarter of the breadcrumb mixture. Arrange the tuna slices on top of this and spread over the pesto. Sprinkle with another quarter of the breadcrumb mixture. Arrange the tomatoes over the tuna and pesto, season and sprinkle with another quarter of the breadcrumb mixture.

Roll or pull the remaining dough into an 27-cm/11-inch circle. Brush the edge of the dough with a little water. Lay the circle of dough over the pie and press the edges to seal. Trim off the excess dough with a sharp knife. Brush the top with olive oil and sprinkle with the remaining breadcrumb mixture. Make 2 slashes in the centre of the pie. Bake in the oven for 35–45 minutes until golden. Serve warm or cold.

BURRATA, POTATO, SAGE AND RED ONION MARMELLATA PIZZA PIE

Torta salata con burrata, patate, salvia e marmellata di cipolle dolci

½ recipe Basic Pizza Dough (page 12)

400 g/14 oz. potatoes

250 g/9 oz. burrata cheese

2–3 fresh sage or rosemary sprigs, broken into small pieces

bitter radicchio/Italian chicory and rocket/arugula salad, to serve

RED ONION MARMELLATA (MAKES ABOUT 500 G/18 OZ.):

800 g/1¾ lbs. red onions, thinly sliced

75 g/½ cup sultanas/golden raisins

150 g/¾ cup light soft brown sugar

75 g/⅓ cup golden caster/granulated sugar

50 ml/3½ tablespoons red wine

50 ml/3½ tablespoons red wine vinegar

2 teaspoons chopped fresh thyme

2 whole cloves

sea salt and freshly ground black pepper

a pizza pan or springform cake pan, 25 cm/10 inches and 4 cm/1¾ inches deep, lightly oiled

MAKES 1 PIE (25 CM/10 INCHES)

This is a ridiculously indulgent winter warmer oozing melted cheese. I sometimes sprinkle rinsed salted capers over the cheese to cut through the richness of it. Meat eaters could add crispy fried lardons of bacon in with the potatoes. You will have enough onion marmellata to use for other things – it's delicious with salty cheeses.

First make the red onion marmellata, put the sliced onions in a heavy casserole dish. Add the sultanas/golden raisins, sugars, wine, vinegar, thyme and cloves, season with salt and pepper, stir well, cover and leave to marinate for at least 2 hours or overnight. Cook over a medium heat for about 1 hour, stirring every now and then to prevent it catching. Watch carefully during the last 15 minutes of cooking that it doesn't catch and burn. It is ready when thick and there is no more liquid. Spoon into a screw-top jar with a layer of olive oil on top to exclude the air. This will keep for 3 months in a cool place.

Put a baking sheet in the middle of the oven. Preheat the oven to 200°C (400°F) Gas 6.

Meanwhile, put the potatoes in a pan of salted water and bring to the boil. Cook for 10 minutes, or until tender. Drain, then slice thickly.

Uncover the dough, punch out the air and roll into a rough 35-cm/14-inch circle. Use this to line the prepared pizza pan, draping extra dough over the edge if necessary. Scatter half the burrata over the base, followed by blobs of onion marmellata, the sliced potatoes and finally the remaining cheese. Sprinkle with rosemary or sage. Trim around the edge with a sharp knife and discard the excess dough.

Slide into the oven on top of the baking sheet and bake for 25–35 minutes until bubbling with a golden crust.

Remove from the oven and leave to stand for 10 minutes before serving in thick wedges.

Serve with a bitter radicchio and rocket salad to complement the rich filling.

ITALIAN SAUSAGE, POTATO AND RICOTTA DOUBLE-CRUST SFINCIUNE

Sfinciune al salsicce e patate

1 recipe Sicilian Pizza Dough (page 16)

2 tablespoons extra virgin olive oil, plus extra to glaze

200 g/7 oz. potatoes, peeled and finely diced

2 onions, finely chopped

1 teaspoon dried oregano

250 g/9 oz. fresh Italian sausage, peeled

1 teaspoon fennel seeds

2 tablespoons chopped fresh sage

125 g/4 oz. ricotta

sea salt and freshly ground black pepper

a testo, terracotta baking stone or a large, heavy baking sheet

a rimless baking sheet

MAKES 1 DOUBLE-CRUST PIZZA (30 CM/12 INCHES)

This double-crust pizza was made famous by the nuns of San Vito lo Capo in Sicily. My version contains ricotta and is a true meat feast. I regularly make it when I am teaching in Sicily. We have a special pizza day when we make doughs and toppings then head for the farmhouse with its antique bread oven. This is the first pizza we make and we waste no time tucking into it.

Place the testo, baking stone or a large, heavy baking sheet on the lower shelf of the oven. Preheat the oven to 220°C (425°F) Gas 7 for at least 30 minutes.

Heat the oil in a frying pan/skillet and add the potatoes and onions. Cook for 5–10 minutes until the onion starts to colour and the potato is soft. Stir in the oregano. Season, then transfer to a bowl to cool. Fry the sausage briefly in the same frying pan/skillet, breaking it up with the back of a fork. Add the fennel seeds and sage and fry for a couple of minutes – but not too long or the meat will toughen. Season well, then let cool.

Uncover the dough, knock out the air and divide into 2. Roll each piece into a thin, 30-cm/12-inch circle directly onto baking parchment. Spread the potato and onion mixture onto one circle, leaving a 1-cm/3/8-inch rim around the edge. Dot with the sausage and the cheese. Season. Brush the edge with water and lay the remaining circle on top. Pinch and roll the edges to seal. Brush with a little olive oil. Make 2 slashes in the centre of the pie, then slide onto the rimless baking sheet.

Working quickly, open the oven door and slide paper and pizza onto the hot baking stone or baking sheet. If you are brave, try to shoot the pizza into the oven so that it leaves the paper behind – this takes practice!

Bake for 10 minutes, then carefully slide out the baking parchment. Bake the pizza for a further 25–30 minutes, or until the crust is puffed up and golden. Remove from the oven and brush with a little olive oil. Let stand for 5 minutes before serving. Eat hot, warm or cold.

ROLLED PESTO, OLIVE AND GARLIC BREAD

Rotolo di pane con olive, aglio e basilica

This is almost an Italian equivalent of hot garlic bread, but much better. You can use ordinary pizza dough, or enrich it with egg. The thin dough crust is smothered in pesto and green olives, rolled up to look like a long jelly roll and left to rise again. Drenched in garlic oil and smothered in pecorino, the smell alone wafting from the oven is to die for!

Sift the flour, sugar and salt into a large bowl and make a well in the centre. Crumble in the compressed yeast or sprinkle in the active dry yeast, if using. If you are using quick-rising yeast, follow the manufacturer's instructions. Rub in the yeast until the mixture resembles fine breadcrumbs. Pour in the beaten egg, olive oil and the hand-hot water and mix until the dough comes together. Knead the dough energetically, on a floured surface, for 5 minutes until soft, smooth and elastic. Put it in a lightly oiled bowl, cover with clingfilm/plastic wrap or a damp kitchen towel and let rise in a warm place until doubled in size – about 1¹/₂ hours.

Place the testo, baking stone or a large, heavy baking sheet on the lower shelf of the oven. Preheat the oven to 200°C (400°F) Gas 6.

When risen, knock back the dough, then roll or pull into a large rectangle as thinly as you can, directly onto a sheet of baking parchment. Spread the dough liberally with the pesto, leaving a 1-cm/³/₈-inch rim all around the dough, then scatter over the olives and 125 g/1³/₄ cups of the pecorino. Season. Using the baking parchment, roll the dough up like a Swiss/jelly roll, starting from the long side. Slide the dough onto another sheet of parchment, making sure the seam is underneath. Brush with the garlic oil and sprinkle with the remaining pecorino.

Slide the rolled bread onto the pizza peel or rimless baking sheet. Working quickly, open the oven door and slide paper and bread onto the hot baking stone or baking sheet.

Bake for 20 minutes, then carefully slide out the baking parchment. Bake for a further 5 minutes until the crust is golden and the cheese melted. Remove from the oven and serve warm (not hot) or cold in slices.

1 recipe Classic Pesto Genovese (page 20)

500 g/4¼ cups Italian '0' or '00' flour, or unbleached plain/all-purpose flour

1 teaspoon sugar

½ teaspoon fine sea salt

25 g/1 cake compressed yeast, 1 tablespoon/1 packet active dry yeast, or 2 teaspoons fast-action dried yeast

1 egg, beaten

3 tablespoons extra virgin olive oil

350 ml/1²/₃ cups hand-hot water

200 g/7 oz. large green olives, stoned/pitted and roughly chopped

200 g/3 cups freshly grated pecorino or Parmesan cheese

2–3 tablespoons garlic-infused olive oil

sea salt and freshly ground black pepper

a testo, terracotta baking stone or a large, heavy baking sheet

a pizza peel or rimless baking sheet

SERVES 6 AS A LOAF

WALNUT AND PARSLEY ROLLS

Sfogliate ai noci e prezzemolo

1 recipe Basic Pizza Dough (page 12)

200 g/1½ cups walnut pieces

1 handful of fresh parsley leaves

2 garlic cloves

100 ml/⅓ cup extra virgin olive oil

sea salt and freshly ground
black pepper

*a deep pizza pan or springform cake
pan, 23 cm/9 inches, lightly oiled*

**MAKES ABOUT
20 SMALL ROLLS**

These are delicious little savoury rolls made just like British Chelsea buns and baked together in a pan. Take the whole lot to the dinner table and break off your own little roll. Perfect with drinks on a hot summer night, or instead of bread, they disappear very fast!

Preheat the oven to 200°C (400°F) Gas 6.

Put the walnuts, parsley and garlic in a food processor and process until evenly chopped. While the machine is running, pour in the olive oil. Season to taste.

Uncover the dough, punch out the air and roll or pull into a rectangle, 60 x 20 cm/24 x 8 inches, directly onto a large sheet of baking parchment.

Spread the walnut mixture over the dough. Season. Using the baking parchment, roll the dough up like a Swiss/jelly roll, starting from the long side. Slide the dough onto another sheet of parchment, making sure the seam is underneath. Using a very sharp knife cut the roll into 20 even pieces. Cut the dough quickly and smoothly each time – don't saw it or it will stick! Arrange the rolls cut-side up in the prepared pizza pan, spacing them close together but not quite touching. Cover with oiled clingfilm/plastic wrap or a damp kitchen towel and let rise to the top of the pan for about 30 minutes.

Remove the clingfilm/plastic wrap and bake the rolls for 35–45 minutes or until golden. Let cool in the pan if you want them very soft, or turn them out onto a rack to cool if you'd like them drier. Serve warm.

DOUGH BALLS

Panizze

1 recipe Basic Pizza Dough (page 12) or Sicilian Pizza Dough (page 16)

1 tablespoon fine sea salt

ricotta, marinated aubergine/eggplant, and canned tuna, to serve

a large baking sheet lined with baking parchment

MAKES 12 BALLS

We all love bread dough, but often the dough balls in pizza restaurants are just too heavy. This is my version – little balls of pizza dough washed with a salty glaze. Split them while they are still hot, pull out the doughy centre and fill with cool, creamy ricotta, a spoonful of aubergine/eggplant antipasto and some good canned tuna in oil.

Preheat the oven to 200°C (400°F) Gas 6.

Uncover the dough, punch out the air and divide it into 12. Shape each piece into a neat ball.

Put the dough balls on the prepared baking sheet, spacing them well apart. Cover loosely with a sheet of lightly oiled clingfilm/plastic wrap or a damp kitchen towel and let rise again until doubled in size – about 30 minutes.

Dissolve the salt in 3 tablespoons water. When the dough balls have risen, brush them with the salt solution.

Bake the rolls for 15–20 minutes until risen and brown. Cool on a wire rack then split and fill with the ricotta, aubergine/eggplant and tuna.

PIZZA POCKETS

Pagnotielli

½ recipe Basic Pizza Dough (page 12), making just 1 ball of dough

cooked sliced ham, sliced tomatoes, sliced mozzarella and rocket/arugula, or other filling of choice, to serve

a terracotta baking stone or a large, heavy baking sheet

MAKES 4–6 PIZZA POCKETS, DEPENDING ON SIZE

This is a revelation! If you like baking, then try these – they are very easy to make, versatile (make them any shape or size you like) and the result is so professional. Indeed, they are becoming a very popular snack. Once baked, they can be frozen and reheated, as long as they are wrapped in foil to keep them moist. They must be warm when they are split or they will crack.

Place the baking stone or a large heavy baking sheet on the lower shelf of the oven. Preheat the oven to 220°C (425°F) Gas 7 for at least 30 minutes.

Uncover the dough, punch out the air and divide it into 6 (or however many you wish). Shape each piece into a round ball then roll out to an oval. Using a fork with large tines, prick them all over (but not too much).

Lay the pizza pockets on 2 sheets of lightly floured baking parchment. If they don't all fit, bake them in batches.

Working quickly, open the oven door and slide the paper onto the hot baking stone or baking sheet.

Bake for 3–5 minutes, until very puffed up and very pale golden. Remove from the oven and wrap in a clean kitchen towel to keep warm and soft if you need to cook another batch.

When they are all cooked, quickly cut them in half across the middle and open out the pocket. Stuff with your chosen filling, for example cooked ham, tomato and mozzarella. Wrap loosely in foil, then return to the oven for 2 minutes. Unwrap, add rocket/arugula and eat immediately.

FOCACCIA

DEEP-PAN FOCACCIA

Focaccia alta

750 g/6⅓ cups Italian '00' flour or cake flour, plus extra as necessary

½ teaspoon fine sea salt

25 g/1 cake compressed yeast, 1 tablespoon/1 packet active dry yeast, or 2 teaspoons fast-action dried yeast

150 ml/⅔ cup extra virgin olive oil

400–450 ml/1¾–2 cups hand-hot water

coarse sea salt

fresh rosemary sprigs (optional)

2 cake, pie or pizza pans, 25 cm/10 inches and 4 cm/1½ inches deep, lightly oiled

MAKES 2 FOCACCIAS (25 CM/10 INCHES)

The word focaccia means a bread baked directly on the hearth and derives from the Latin word for 'hearth' (*focus*). In Ligurian dialect focaccia is known as fugassa from which the French word fougasse originates. Although a rustic focaccia can be made with any basic pizza dough, the secret of a truly light, thick focaccia lies in giving the dough three risings and dimpling the dough so that it traps olive oil while it bakes. Follow the instructions on page 17 for shaping the bread.

Sift the flour and fine sea salt into a large bowl and make a well in the centre. Crumble in the compressed yeast, or add active dry yeast, if using. If you are using quick-rising active yeast, follow the manufacturer's instructions. Pour in 50 ml/3½ tablespoons of the olive oil, then rub in the yeast until the mixture resembles fine breadcrumbs. Pour in the hand-hot water and mix together with your hands until the dough comes together.

Tip the dough out onto a floured surface, wash and dry your hands and knead energetically for 10 minutes until smooth and elastic. The dough should be very soft (almost too soft to handle), but don't worry about it too much at this stage.

Put the dough in a lightly oiled bowl, cover with clingfilm/plastic wrap or a damp kitchen towel and let rise in a warm place until doubled in size – about 1½ hours.

Uncover the dough, punch out the air and divide into 2. Shape each piece into a round ball on a lightly floured surface and roll out into two 25-cm/10-inch circles and place in the pans. Cover with clingfilm/plastic wrap or a damp kitchen towel and let rise for 30 minutes.

Preheat the oven to 200°C (400°F) Gas 6.

Follow the instructions on page 17 for shaping your bread.

Spray the focaccias with water and bake for 20–25 minutes until risen and golden. Drizzle with the remaining olive oil then transfer to a wire rack to cool.

Eat on the same day or let cool, then wrap up and freeze. When you remove the focaccia from the freezer, thaw and wrap in foil, then reheat for 5 minutes in a hot oven.

THIN FOCACCIA

Focaccia bassa

This is a wonderful example of the traditional focaccia, as it is baked directly on the baking stone or on a hot baking sheet. If the dough is floured very well the focaccia can be slipped directly onto the stone or baking sheet, leaving the baking parchment behind. This is the kind of focaccia that you tear and dip into yet more fruity olive oil.

1 recipe Deep-pan Focaccia
(page 100), risen twice but uncooked

100 ml/⅓ cup extra virgin olive oil

coarse sea salt

*2 testi, terracotta baking stones
or large, heavy baking sheets*

*2 rimless baking sheets, lined with
baking parchment*

**MAKES 2 LARGE,
THIN FOCACCIAS**

Put the 2 testi, baking stones or large, heavy baking sheets on the lower shelf of the oven. Preheat the oven to 220°C (425°F) Gas 7 for at least 30 minutes.

Uncover the dough, punch out the air and divide into 2. Shape each piece into a rough ball then pull and stretch the dough to a large oval shape – as large as will fit in your oven. Place on the rimless baking sheets. Cover with lightly oiled clingfilm/plastic wrap or a damp kitchen towel and let rise for 30 minutes.

Remove the clingfilm/plastic wrap and, using your fingertips, make deep dimples all over the surface of the dough right down to the baking sheet. Drizzle over all but 2 tablespoons of the remaining oil. Spray the focaccias with water and sprinkle generously with salt. Working quickly, open the oven door and slide paper and focaccia onto the hot baking stones or baking sheets.

Bake for 15 minutes, then carefully slide out the baking parchment. Bake the focaccia for a further 15 minutes, or until the crust is golden. Brush or drizzle with the remaining olive oil then transfer to a wire rack to cool. Eat on the same day or let cool, then wrap up and freeze. When you remove it from the freezer, thaw and wrap in foil, then reheat for 5 minutes in a hot oven.

STUFFED FOCACCIA WITH FIGS, PROSCIUTTO AND TALEGGIO

Focaccia farcita

½ recipe Deep-pan Focaccia (page 100), making just 1 focaccia

3 tablespoons extra virgin olive oil

6 fresh ripe figs, quartered or sliced

6 slices prosciutto

125 g/4 oz. Taleggio or Gorgonzola cheese, sliced

sea salt and freshly ground black pepper

**MAKES 1 FOCACCIA
(25 CM/10 INCHES)**

This is just the thing to make when there are very good fresh figs around – you will be very popular, as this is just heavenly! The combination of sweet juicy figs, salty ham and rich, runny Taleggio is heady stuff. Mozzarella and Gorgonzola would both work well here (you need a soft melting cheese) and I've even made it using overripe peaches instead of figs.

Bake the focaccia without the rosemary following the recipe on page 100. Remove from the oven and tip out of the pan.

Holding the hot focaccia in a kitchen towel to protect your hands, slice through it horizontally with a serrated knife.

Brush the insides with the olive oil. Fill with the figs, prosciutto and Taleggio, seasoning as you go. Put the top back on and wrap loosely in foil, then return to the hot oven for 5 minutes. Unwrap, cut into thick wedges and eat while warm and melting.

FIERY FOCACCIA

Focaccia alla diavola

This is a good focaccia for making outrageous sandwiches or serving in thick slices smothered in fresh ricotta. Replacing some of the liquid in the dough with tomato paste (or even all the water with tomato juice) gives it a beautiful, rusty red colour, studded with bright red (bell) pepper and dark chunks of salami or chorizo.

½ recipe Deep-pan Focaccia (page 100), making the changes stated in this recipe

4 tablespoons tomato purée/paste

4–6 red chillies/cherry peppers or Peppadews, diced

2 red (bell) peppers, roasted, seeded and diced

100 g/3½ oz. *salame piccante* or chorizo, cubed

75 g/2½ oz. *provolone piccante*, Emmental or Gruyère cheese, cubed

100 ml/⅓ cup extra virgin olive oil, plus extra to glaze

coarse sea salt and freshly ground black pepper

a cake or pizza pan, 25 cm/10 inches and 4 cm/1½ inches deep, lightly oiled

MAKES 1 FOCACCIA
(25 CM/10 INCHES)

Make the focaccia dough following the recipe on page 100, but using 4 tablespoons tomato purée/paste dissolved in the water. Knead the dough and give it the first rising.

Uncover the dough, punch out the air and pull or roll it out into a rough circle. Dot with the chillies/cherry peppers, red (bell) peppers, salami, provolone and lots of freshly ground black pepper. Flip one half of the dough over and lightly knead to incorporate the ingredients. Shape into a rough ball on a lightly floured surface and pat into the prepared pan. Cover lightly with clingfilm/plastic wrap or a damp kitchen towel and let rise for 30 minutes.

Remove the clingfilm/plastic wrap and, using your fingertips, make deep dimples all over the surface of the dough. Drizzle over the olive oil, re-cover very lightly with clingfilm/plastic wrap and let rise for a final 30 minutes until very puffy.

Preheat the oven to 200°C (400°F) Gas 6.

Uncover the focaccia, mist with water and sprinkle generously with salt. Bake for 20–25 minutes until risen and golden. Transfer to a wire rack, brush with olive oil and let cool. Eat on the same day or let cool, then wrap up and freeze. When you remove it from the freezer, thaw and wrap in foil, then reheat for 5 minutes in a hot oven.

CORNMEAL AND OLIVE FOCACCIA WITH ROSEMARY AND SAGE

La marocca

This is an unusual bread from the coastal areas of Lunigiana and made from a mixture of cornmeal and wheat flour. It is traditionally made between November and the end of January to coincide with the olive harvest. It is cooked in a wood-fired oven on a bed of chestnut leaves and takes on a deep brown crust.

500 g/4¼ cups Italian '00' flour or cake flour

300 g/2¼ cups fine polenta flour (*farina gialla* or *granoturco*)

2 x 7-g/¼-oz. sachets fast-action dried yeast

200 g/7 oz. black olives, stoned/pitted and halved

3 tablespoons pine nuts

2 tablespoons chopped fresh sage

2 tablespoons chopped fresh rosemary

2–3 garlic cloves, finely chopped

3 tablespoons extra virgin olive oil, plus extra to drizzle

450 ml/2 cups hand-hot water

coarse sea salt and freshly ground black pepper

a Swiss/jelly roll pan, 33 x 23 cm/ 13 x 9 inches, oiled

MAKES 1 FOCACCIA
(33 X 23 CM/13 X 9 INCHES)

Mix the flours and yeast in a large bowl. Add the olives, pine nuts, sage, rosemary and garlic, then mix. Make a well in the centre and add the olive oil mixed with the hand-hot water. Mix to a very soft dough, turn out onto a lightly floured work surface and knead very vigorously for 10 minutes.

Roll or pull the dough into a rectangle to fit the Swiss/jelly roll pan, pushing the dough into the corners. Cover with clingfilm/plastic wrap or a damp kitchen towel and let rise in a warm place for about 20–30 minutes until quite puffy.

Meanwhile, preheat the oven to 200°C (400°F) Gas 6.

Using your fingertips, make deep dimples all over the dough and drizzle with olive oil. Sprinkle with salt and bake for about 35 minutes, until risen, firm and dark golden.

TRUFFLED BREAKFAST FOCACCIA

Focaccia tartufata con pancetta

½ recipe Deep-pan Focaccia (page 100), making just 1 ball of dough, up to the first rising

4 tablespoons extra virgin olive oil, plus extra to fry

a few drops of good truffle oil

100 g/6½ tablespoons unsalted butter, melted

12 thin slices pancetta or bacon

4 eggs

sea salt and freshly ground black pepper

4 deep, springform cake pans, 12 cm/5 inches each, lightly oiled

MAKES 4 FOCACCIAS
(12 CM/5 INCHES)

Now here's something to start the day properly. Little warm focaccias are split, the insides brushed with a few drops of truffle oil mixed with melted butter and filled with crispy fried pancetta and a fried egg. A real special-occasion dish. Be careful when you use truffle oil, as it can be overpowering; and be sure to use real truffle-infused oil not the artificially flavoured variety.

Uncover the dough, punch out the air and divide into 4. Shape each piece into a round ball on a lightly floured surface. Roll out into 12-cm/5-inch circles and place in the prepared cake pans. Cover with clingfilm/plastic wrap or a damp kitchen towel and let rise for 30 minutes.

Preheat the oven to 200°C (400°F) Gas 6.

Using your fingertips, make deep dimples all over the dough right to the base of the pans and drizzle with the olive oil. Re-cover and let rise to the top of the pans – about 30 minutes.

Spray the focaccias with water, sprinkle generously with salt and bake for 20–25 minutes until risen and golden.

While the focaccias are baking, mix the truffle oil with the melted butter and keep warm. Grill the pancetta until crisp – or bake in the oven at the same time as the focaccia. Fry the eggs in olive oil and keep warm.

When the focaccias are ready, tip them out of their pans, hold them in a kitchen towel to protect your hands and slice through them horizontally with a serrated knife. (If they seem too thick, shave a slice off the inside.) Brush the insides with the truffle butter and lay three pancetta slices and an egg on each one. Replace the tops and serve immediately.

To make the focaccias ahead of time, bake them and let cool, then wrap up and freeze. When you remove them from the freezer, thaw and wrap in foil, then reheat for 5 minutes in a hot oven.

POTATO AND OLIVE FOCACCIA

Focaccia con patate e olive

500 g/1 lb. baking potatoes, unpeeled

600 g/5¼ cups Italian '00' flour or plain/all-purpose flour, plus extra as necessary

½ teaspoon fine sea salt

25 g/1 cake compressed fresh yeast, 1 tablespoon/1 packet active dry yeast, or 2 teaspoons fast-action dried yeast

200 g/7 oz. large, juicy green olives, stones/pits in

150 ml/⅔ cup extra virgin olive oil

coarse sea salt

2 cake pans, 25 cm/10 inches and 4 cm/1½ inches deep or a large rectangular pan, lightly oiled

**MAKES 2 FOCACCIAS
(25 CM/10 INCHES)**

Making a bread by mixing mashed potatoes with flour and anointing it lavishly with good olive oil is common all over Italy, especially in Liguria and Puglia, where some of the best olive oils come from. Sometimes, the top is covered in paper-thin slices of potato and scattered with rosemary before baking. Either way it is delicious, but quite dense. I tend not to stone/pit the olives for this as they can dry out too much in the oven.

Boil or bake the potatoes in their skins and peel them while still warm. Mash them or pass them through a potato ricer.

Sift the flour with the fine salt into a large bowl and make a well in the centre. Crumble in the compressed yeast or add active dry yeast, if using. If using fast-action dried yeast, follow the manufacturer's instructions.

Add the potatoes and mix together with your hands until the dough comes together. Tip the dough out onto a floured surface, wash and dry your hands, and knead energetically for 10 minutes until smooth and elastic. The dough should be soft; if it isn't, add a couple of tablespoons warm water.

Divide the dough into 2, shape each piece into a round ball on a lightly floured surface, and roll out into two 25-cm/10-inch circles or a large rectangle to fit whichever pan you are using. Put the dough in the pan, cover with clingfilm/plastic wrap or a damp kitchen towel, and let rise for 2 hours.

Preheat the oven to 200°C (400°F) Gas 6. Uncover the dough, scatter over the olives and, using your fingertips, make deep dimples all over the surface of the dough, pushing in some of the olives here and there. Drizzle with two-thirds of the olive oil, re-cover and let rise for another 30 minutes.

Uncover the dough, spray with water and sprinkle generously with salt. Bake for 20–25 minutes until risen and golden brown. Brush or drizzle with the remaining olive oil then transfer to a wire rack to cool. Eat on the same day, or let cool, wrap up and freeze. When you remove the focaccia from the freezer, thaw and wrap in foil, then reheat for 5 minutes in a hot oven.

OAT FLOUR FOCACCIA

Focaccia al avena

2½ teaspoons/1 packet fast-action dried yeast

1 teaspoon sugar

350–450 ml/1⅔–2 cups hand-hot water

125 g/1 cup oat flour, warmed

500 g/4¼ cups Italian '00' flour or cake flour, warmed

2 teaspoons English mustard powder

1 teaspoon freshly ground black pepper

2 teaspoons fine salt

2 tablespoons extra virgin olive oil, plus extra to drizzle

3–4 tablespoons old-fashioned rolled oats

coarse sea salt

2 Swiss/jelly roll pans, 23 x 32 cm/ 9 x 13 inches

MAKES 2 THIN, RECTANGULAR FOCACCIAS

When I was teaching in Italy, I made focaccia in all shapes and sizes and with many different flours. I wondered how it would taste if I incorporated my native oat flour. I decided to use fine oat flour and Italian '00' flour and to scatter rolled oats and salt on top. The result was a thin, crisp and moist focaccia, with a golden, crunchy topping. Make sure all the ingredients are at warm room temperature and if necessary, warm them in a low oven – this will help the dough to rise.

Beat the yeast and sugar into the hand-hot water and stir in the warmed oat flour. Cover and let stand in a warm place for 10–15 minutes until frothy.

Sift the Italian '00' flour, mustard powder, pepper and fine salt into a warm bowl, pour in the oat flour mixture and add the olive oil. Mix to a soft dough. Add a little extra warm water if the dough looks too dry. Turn out and knead for at least 10 minutes or until elastic (see page 17).

Place in a lightly oiled bowl, cover with clingfilm/plastic wrap or a damp kitchen towel and let rise in a warm place for about 1 hour or until doubled in size.

Uncover the dough, punch out the air and divide in 2. Pull and roll each piece to fit the Swiss/jelly roll pans. Place in the pans and press into the corners. Prick the dough all over with a fork and scatter the rolled oats and coarse sea salt over the top. Cover with oiled clingfilm/plastic wrap or a damp kitchen towel and let rise until puffy – 30–60 minutes.

Preheat the oven to 200°C (400°F) Gas 6.

Drizzle the focaccias with olive oil and bake for 25 minutes until golden. Remove from the oven and drizzle with a little more olive oil. Cool on a wire rack and serve cut into thin fingers. Best eaten the same day.

RICOTTA AND PROSCIUTTO FOCACCIA

Torta di focaccia con ricotta e prosciutto crudo

½ recipe Deep-pan Focaccia (page 100), making just 1 ball of dough, up to the first rising

4 eggs

100 g/6 tablespoons ricotta

6 tablespoons chopped fresh parsley or rocket/arugula

55 g/½ cup freshly grated pecorino cheese

150 g/5 oz. thinly sliced prosciutto

extra virgin olive oil, to glaze

freshly ground black pepper

a pizza pan or springform cake pan, 23 cm/9 inches and 4 cm/1½ inches deep, lightly oiled

MAKES 1 FOCACCIA
(23 CM/9 INCHES)

Doesn't focaccia have to have dimples? Well, in general it does but it varies depending on where you live in Italy. This recipe merits being a focaccia because it is made with an olive oil-enriched dough and it has a filling, like so many focaccias. It's the Italian equivalent of bacon and egg pie but it's made with lots of parsley and lovely fresh ricotta.

Preheat the oven to 220°C (425°F) Gas 7 for at least 30 minutes.

While the dough rises, make the filling. Put the eggs, ricotta and parsley in a food processor and process until smooth. Pour into a jug/pitcher and mix in the pecorino. Season with pepper but no salt.

Uncover the dough, punch out the air and knead until smooth. Roll two-thirds of it into a 32-cm/13-inch circle and use this to line the pizza pan, draping the extra dough over the edge. Alternate layers of prosciutto and ricotta mixture until they are all used up.

Roll the remaining dough into a 27-cm/11-inch circle. Brush the edge of the filled dough with water. Lift the circle of dough over the pie and press the edges to seal. Trim off the excess dough with a sharp knife. Brush with olive oil. Make 2 slashes in the centre of the pie. Bake for 20–25 minutes until golden. Serve warm or cold.

Oozing cheese pizza

Focaccia con formaggio

250 g/2 cups plus 2 tablespoons Italian '00' flour or cake flour

100 ml/6 tablespoons warm water

3 tablespoons extra virgin olive oil, plus extra to glaze

5 balls cow's milk mozzarella (*fior di latte*) or a smoked mozzarella, which will be firmer

6 tablespoons dried breadcrumbs

sea salt

a testo, terracotta baking stone or a large, heavy baking sheet

a rimless baking sheet

MAKES 1 FOCACCIA, 30 CM/12 INCHES

This amazing focaccia features the reverse of dimpling – cobbles, which ooze cheese when they are cut open. The dough is made with olive oil and has no yeast in it. The secret is to roll out the dough very thinly so that it cooks quickly and hasn't got time to absorb the melting cheese. The breadcrumbs are there to absorb any whey escaping from the cheese.

First, make an unleavened dough by mixing the flour, the warm water and the olive oil. Add more warm water if necessary. Knead well until smooth and elastic, then place in a bowl, cover and let rest for 1 hour.

Put the testo, baking stone or a large, heavy baking sheet on the lower shelf of the oven. Preheat the oven to 220°C (425°F) Gas 7 for at least 30 minutes.

Divide the dough into 2, making one piece slightly larger than the other. Using plenty of flour for dusting, roll the larger piece as thinly as you can into a 30-cm/12-inch circle directly onto baking parchment and slide onto a rimless baking sheet.

Cut the mozzarella balls in half and lightly squeeze out any moisture. Dip the bases in the dried breadcrumbs. Arrange the cheeses, domed-side up, over the crust, adding any remaining breadcrumbs underneath each one. Roll out the remaining dough as thinly as you can and slightly larger than the crust. Lift this over the cheeses and gently press the dough down and around each piece of cheese. The blunt edge of a cookie cutter will help you to seal the edge of each mound – use a cutter that fits just around a mound. Make sure there are no holes for the cheese to run through. Twist and crimp the edges of the pizza together. Carefully brush with olive oil and sprinkle with salt.

Working quickly, open the oven door and slide paper and pizza onto the hot baking stone or baking sheet. If you are brave, try to shoot the pizza into the oven so that it leaves the paper behind – this takes practice!

Bake for 10–15 minutes or until golden, then remove from the oven and serve immediately, cut with a pizza wheel into oozing wedges.

EASTER CHEESE FOCACCIA

Torta pasquale

25 g/1 cake compressed fresh yeast

200 ml/¾ cup hand-hot water

a pinch of sugar

4 eggs (at room temperature), beaten

500 g/4¼ cups Italian '00' flour or cake flour

100 g/1 cup freshly grated Parmesan cheese

sea salt and freshly ground black pepper

relish or pesto, to serve

a ring mould, 23 cm/9 inches, oiled and dusted with flour

MAKES 1 RING (23 CM/9 INCHES)

This unusual cheese loaf is baked in a ring mould because the dough is made from a loose batter – almost a brioche – and the mould will hold it nicely. This sort of bread is normally only made for holidays and celebrations, but it's delicious toasted for breakfast; the smell will rouse even the sleepiest member of the household. The bread can easily be baked in a loaf pan but it is not quite as pretty.

Dissolve the yeast in the hand-hot water with the sugar. Beat in the eggs. Put the flour and Parmesan in an electric mixer and season. Pour in the yeast mixture and mix slowly, on a low setting, for 5 minutes until smooth. Turn up to medium and mix for a further 5 minutes. The batter should be very soft. Pour or scoop the batter into the prepared ring mould, cover with a damp kitchen towel and let rise for 1 hour or until puffy.

Preheat the oven to 180°C (350°F) Gas 4.

Bake the dough in the oven for 35–40 minutes until well risen and a deep, rich brown on top. Invert onto a wire rack and let stand for 10 minutes in the mould. Lift off the mould, turn the bread over and cool. Serve, in slices, with relish or pesto.

PARMESAN SODA BREAD

Torta reggiano

This is an unyeasted bread from Umbria and very quick to rustle up. Little packets of baking powder are especially made for instant savoury doughs in Italy. When making this type of bread, work quickly, because as soon as the liquid comes into contact with the baking powder, a chemical reaction starts to aerate the bread. Use a light hand and get the dough into the oven as soon as possible.

300 g/2⅔ cups Italian '00' flour
or cake flour

1 teaspoon baking powder

1 teaspoon salt

50 g/½ cup freshly grated
Parmesan cheese, plus extra to dust

50 g/3 tablespoons butter,
melted and cooled

100–150 ml/½–⅔ cup milk

2 medium eggs

a testo, terracotta baking stone
or a large, heavy baking sheet

a rimless baking sheet,
lined with baking parchment

MAKES 1 LOAF
(APPROXIMATELY
23 CM/9 INCHES)

Put the testo, baking stone or a large, heavy baking sheet on the lower shelf of the oven. Preheat the oven to 190°C (375°F) Gas 5 for at least 30 minutes.

Sift the flour, baking powder and salt into a medium mixing bowl. Stir in the Parmesan and make a well in the centre.

Beat the cooled, melted butter with 100 ml/½ cup of the milk and the eggs and pour into the well. Mix until *just* combined – overmixing will make the bread tough. The dough should be quite soft; if it isn't, add a little more milk. Turn out onto a floured work surface and knead briefly. Put the ball of dough directly onto a rimless baking sheet lined with baking parchment. Pat into a disk about 3 cm/1¼ inches thick. Brush with a little extra milk, then mark into wedges with the back of a knife and dust with extra Parmesan.

Working quickly, open the oven door and slide paper and bread onto the hot baking stone or baking sheet. If you are brave, try to shoot the bread into the oven so that it leaves the paper behind – this takes practice!

Bake for 15 minutes, then carefully slide out the baking parchment. Bake for a further 5 minutes or until the crust is really golden. Remove from the oven and wrap in a kitchen towel. Serve warm, broken into wedges, ready to split and fill.

CORNMEAL MUFFINS

Focaccette di granoturco

25 g/1 cake compressed fresh yeast,
1 tablespoon/1 packet active dry yeast,
or 2 teaspoons fast-action dried yeast

1 teaspoon sugar

400 ml/1¾ cups hand-hot water

500 g/4¼ cups Italian '00' flour
or plain/all-purpose flour

200 g/1⅔ cups fine cornmeal
or polenta

1½ teaspoons fine sea salt

6 tablespoons extra virgin olive oil

*a testo or heavy-based frying pan/
skillet*

MAKES 8 MUFFINS

These little flatbreads are made with cornmeal and wheat flour. They
are similar to English muffins and are served at local *sagre* (festivals) in
the Lunigiana, Tuscany. Cooked on a griddle and ready in minutes, they
are golden and puffy and smell delicious. Fill them with cheese, meat
or salami. You can use polenta for this, but whizz it with the flour in a
food processor to refine it.

In a medium bowl, cream the compressed yeast with the sugar and beat in the
hand-hot water. Leave for 10 minutes until frothy. For other yeasts, follow the
manufacturer's instructions. Sift the flour, cornmeal and salt into a large bowl
and make a well in the centre. Pour in the yeast mixture and the olive oil. Mix
with a round-bladed knife, then your hands, until the dough comes together.

Tip out onto a lightly floured surface, wash and dry your hands (this will
stop the dough sticking to them), then knead briskly for 5–10 minutes until
smooth, shiny and elastic (5 minutes for warm hands, 10 minutes for cold
hands!). Try not to add any extra flour at this stage – a wetter dough is better.
If you feel the dough is sticky, flour your hands and not the dough. The dough
should be quite soft at this point. If it is *really* too soft to handle, knead in a
little more flour.

To test if the dough is ready, roll it into a fat sausage, take each end in either
hand, lift the dough up and pull and stretch the dough outward, gently
wiggling it up and down – it should stretch out quite easily. If it doesn't,
it needs more kneading.

Shape into a neat ball. Place in an oiled bowl, cover with clingfilm/plastic
wrap or a damp kitchen towel and let rise in a warm, draught-free place until
doubled in size – about 1¹/₂ hours. Heat the testo or heavy-based frying pan/
skillet on the stovetop until medium hot.

Uncover the dough, punch out the air, then tip out onto a lightly floured
surface. Divide into 8 smooth balls, then flatten each into a disk about
1-cm/³/₈-inch thick. Slide 2 or 3 disks onto the hot testo or frying pan/skillet
and cook for about 2 minutes on each side, until risen and deep brown on
the underside.

Keep the cooked muffins warm and soft in a cloth or loosely wrapped in foil
in a warm oven while cooking the rest. They are best served warm. Serve split
and filled with cheese, alongside a selection of cold meats and salami.

Chestnut and Vin Santo Focaccia

Focaccia di castagne e Vin Santo

500 g/4¼ cups Italian '00' flour or plain/all-purpose flour

200 g/1⅔ cups chestnut flour (farina di castagne)

1 teaspoon fine sea salt

25 g/1 cake compressed yeast, 1 tablespoon/1 packet active dry yeast, or 2 teaspoons fast-action dried yeast

150 ml/⅔ cup extra virgin olive oil

150 ml/⅔ cup Vin Santo mixed with 300 ml/1⅓ cups water, warmed

coarse sea salt, to sprinkle

2 cake, pie or pizza pans, 25 cm/10 inches and 4 cm/1½ inches deep, lightly oiled

MAKES 2 FOCACCIAS (25 CM/10 INCHES)

Mixing wheat flour with chestnut flour gives this focaccia a wonderful sweet and savoury flavour – almost smoky. It is generally made during the fall or winter months when chestnut flour is readily available and at its best. I serve it with lovely runny Gorgonzola and fresh pears as a dessert – with extra Vin Santo, of course.

Sift the flours and salt into a large bowl and make a well in the centre. Crumble in the compressed yeast. For other yeasts, follow the manufacturer's instructions.

Pour in 3 tablespoons of the olive oil, then rub into the yeast until the mixture resembles fine breadcrumbs. Pour the Vin Santo and water into the well and mix together until the dough comes together.

Tip out onto a lightly floured surface, wash and dry your hands (this will stop the dough sticking to them), then knead briskly for 10 minutes until smooth and elastic. The dough should be very soft, almost too soft to handle, but don't worry at this stage. Put in a lightly oiled bowl, cover with clingfilm/plastic wrap or a damp kitchen towel and let rise in a warm place until doubled – about 1½ hours.

Uncover the dough, punch out the air, then divide into 2. Shape each piece into a round ball on a lightly floured surface. Roll out into 25-cm/10-inch circles and put in the prepared pans. Cover with clingfilm/plastic wrap or a damp kitchen towel and let rise in a warm place for about 45 minutes or until very puffy and almost risen to the top of the pan.

Uncover the dough and, using your fingertips, make deep dimples all over the surface of the dough right to the base of the pan. Drizzle over the remaining oil, re-cover and let rise for a final 30 minutes.

Preheat the oven to 200°C (400°F) Gas 6.

Spray the focaccias with water, lightly sprinkle with salt and bake for 20–25 minutes until risen and golden. Transfer to a wire rack to cool. Eat on the same day or let cool, then wrap up and freeze. When you remove the focaccias from the freezer, thaw and wrap them in foil, then reheat for 5 minutes in a hot oven.

Sticky grape schiacciata

Schiacciata con l'uva

25 g/1 cake compressed fresh yeast,
1 tablespoon/1 packet active dry yeast,
or 2 teaspoons fast-action dried yeast

a pinch of sugar

250 ml/1 cup warm water

500 g/4¼ cups Italian '00' flour
or plain/all-purpose flour

2 egg yolks

2 tablespoons olive oil

½ teaspoon sea salt

175 g/12 tablespoons butter, softened

125 g/½ cup Demerara/brown sugar,
plus extra to sprinkle

finely grated zest of 1 unwaxed lemon

100 g/¾ cup walnuts, chopped

250 g/9 oz. black grapes, seeded
(Sangiovese wine grapes, if possible)

450 ml/2 cups double/heavy cream
or mascarpone

3 tablespoons icing/confectioners'
sugar

100 ml/⅓ cup Vin Santo

*a Swiss/jelly roll pan, 23 x 32 cm/
9 x 13 inches, oiled*

SERVES 6

The word schiacciata literally means 'flattened'. *Schiacciata con l'uva* is a puffy flatbread baked with the Chianti grape (Sangiovese) and sugar and is only seen in bakers' shops at grape harvest time. My sweeter, richer version features black table grapes, walnuts, butter and brown sugar. Instead of grapes, you could use cherries, pine nuts or blueberries, or even raisins soaked overnight in Vin Santo or sherry.

If you are using compressed yeast, mix it with the sugar in a medium bowl, then beat in the warm water. Leave for 10 minutes until frothy. For other yeasts, follow the manufacturer's instructions.

Sift the flour into a large bowl and make a well in the centre. Pour in the yeast mixture, egg yolks, olive oil and salt. Mix until the dough comes together. Tip out onto a lightly floured work surface. Wash and dry your hands. Knead the dough for 10 minutes until smooth and elastic. It should be quite soft, but if it's too soft to handle, add more flour. Place in an oiled bowl, cover with clingfilm/plastic wrap or a damp kitchen towel and let rise until doubled in size – about 1 hour.

To make the walnut butter, cream the butter and Demerara/brown sugar together, then stir in the lemon zest and walnuts. Keep at room temperature.

Uncover the dough, punch out the air, then shape into a ball. Roll or pull the dough into a rectangle to line the prepared Swiss/jelly roll pan. Spread the walnut butter over the schiacciata crust, add the grapes and sprinkle with brown sugar. Cover with clingfilm/plastic wrap or a damp kitchen towel and let rise for 1 hour until puffy and doubled in size.

Preheat the oven to 200°C (400°F) Gas 6. Uncover the dough and bake for 15 minutes. Turn the oven down to 180°C (350°F) Gas 4 and bake for 20 minutes or until risen and golden. Let cool slightly before turning out.

To make the Vin Santo cream, beat the cream, icing/confectioners' sugar and Vin Santo together in a bowl until the mixture forms soft peaks. Cut the focaccia into wedges and serve with the Vin Santo cream.

Sweet Easter Focaccia

Focaccia di pasqua

This focaccia, enriched with egg and butter and infused with saffron, once symbolized wealth and generosity. The dough needs time to rise – the more sugar, butter and eggs in it, the longer it takes. I let it rise slowly in the refrigerator overnight for the main rising, or even the final proving.

25 g/1 cake compressed fresh yeast, 1 tablespoon/1 packet active dry yeast, or 2 teaspoons fast-action dried yeast

a large pinch saffron threads or 2 small packets powdered saffron

150g/¾ cup sugar

200 ml/¾ cup hand-hot water

450 g/3¾ cups Italian '00' flour or plain/all-purpose flour

1 teaspoon salt

5 egg yolks

finely grated zest of 1 unwaxed orange and 1 unwaxed lemon

150 g/10 tablespoons unsalted butter, softened

1 egg, beaten

100 g/1 cup whole blanched almonds

icing/confectioners' sugar, to dredge (optional)

a shallow cake pan, 25 cm/10 inches, oiled

Makes 1 focaccia
(25 cm/10 inches)

Put the yeast and saffron into a large, glass measuring jug/cup and add a teaspoon of the sugar. Mix well, then pour in the hand-hot water and beat until the yeast is dissolved. Leave in a warm place for 10 minutes until frothy.

Whisk 100 g/¾ cup of the flour into the yeast mixture to make a thick, smooth batter. Cover with clingfilm/plastic wrap and let rise in a warm place for about 1 hour until doubled in size. (This could be done overnight in the refrigerator.)

Sift the remaining flour and salt into the bowl of a food mixer. Add the remaining sugar, egg yolks, orange and lemon zest and beat until well mixed. Pour in the batter and beat until smooth and elastic – about 5 minutes. Cover the bowl with clingfilm/plastic wrap and let rise in a warm place until doubled in size – about 2 hours.

Remove the clingfilm/plastic wrap from the batter and gradually beat in the soft butter until shiny and elastic – another 5 minutes. The dough will be very soft. Tip out onto a lightly floured board and shape into a smooth ball. Transfer this to a sheet of baking parchment and roll out into a disk about 2.5 cm/1 inch thick. Cover with an upturned bowl and set aside to prove for 1 hour or until puffy. Alternatively, put the dough in the cake pan and set aside to prove inside the pan.

Preheat the oven to 180°C (350°F) Gas 4.

Once the dough has risen, brush it lightly with the beaten egg and lightly push the almonds randomly into the surface.

Bake for 1 hour until risen and golden. Serve dredged with confectioners' sugar, if using, and with glasses of dessert wine.

FOCACCIA WITH CRISPY KALE WITH WHIPPED RICOTTA, ROASTED GARLIC AND CHIPOTLE

Focaccia con cavolo croccante, crema di ricotta, aglio arrosto e peperoncino chipotle

½ recipe Deep-pan Focaccia (page 100), making just 1 focaccia

100 g/3½ oz. young curly kale or cavolo nero, thinly sliced

4 tablespoons extra virgin olive oil

2–3 garlic cloves, peeled

a 250-g/9-oz. tub ricotta

2 tablespoons whole milk

1–2 teaspoons chipotle powder or purée/paste

6 thin slices chorizo (optional)

sea salt and freshly ground black pepper

a cake pan, pie or pizza pan, 25 cm/10 inches and 4 cm/1½ inches deep, lightly oiled

MAKES 1 FOCACCIA
(25 CM/10 INCHES)

This focaccia is topped with kale or, if you can get it, Italian cavolo nero (from larger supermarkets) which is a type of kale, but very dark in colour. The kale concentrates in flavour as it crisps up almost like Chinese seaweed. Whipping the ricotta with milk and punchy flavourings like garlic and smoky chipotle powder makes it light and meltingly creamy. Serve this as bread with a meal or as a light lunch, with or without the chorizo.

Bake the focaccia without the rosemary following the recipe on page 100. But before you bake it, toss the kale with 2 tablespoons of the olive oil. Scatter this over the top of the focaccia and bake. The kale will brown and crisp.

Meanwhile, boil the garlic cloves in a saucepan of water for 15 minutes until soft. Put the ricotta and milk into a bowl with the garlic and chipotle powder. Using a handheld electric blender, whisk these together at full speed until the ricotta is light and creamy. Taste and season.

When the focaccia is cooked remove from the oven and tip out of the pan.

Holding the hot focaccia in a kitchen towel to protect your hands, slice through it horizontally with a serrated knife. Brush the insides with the remaining olive oil. Fill with the whipped ricotta (and chorizo if using). Put the top back on and rest for 5 minutes. Cut into thick wedges and eat while warm and melting.

TEAR 'N' SHARE 'NDUJA FOCACCIA WITH BASIL AND PRESERVED LEMON DIPPING OIL

Focaccia con 'nduja e con olio alla basilica e limone

1 recipe Basic Pizza Dough (page 12) or Sicilian Pizza Dough (page 16)

200 g/7 oz. 'nduja (spicy Calabrian sausage)

olive oil, to glaze

1 red and 1 green chilli/chile, thinly sliced into rings

1 teaspoon fennel seeds

BASIL AND PRESERVED LEMON OIL:

50 g/2 oz. fresh basil leaves

4–5 tablespoons extra virgin olive oil

25 g/1 oz. chopped preserved lemon

a dash of white wine vinegar (optional)

sea salt and freshly ground black pepper

a shallow rectangular baking pan, 17 x 27 cm/7 x 10½ inches, lightly oiled

MAKES 12 BALLS

Here's something to impress and share with friends – it takes a little patience but is well worth the effort! Once pulled apart, each little bun has a soft fiery salami centre crying out to be dipped in the pungent bright green basil and preserved lemon oil.

Preheat the oven to 200°C (400°F) Gas 6.

Uncover the dough, punch out the air and divide it into 12 equal pieces. Pat or roll out each ball to a flat disk and place a teaspoon of 'nduja on the centre of each one. Bring up the edges over the 'nduja and pinch together in the centre. Flip over and arrange in the oiled pan. Repeat with the remaining dough and 'nduja – don't worry if the balls don't join up in the pan, they will when they have risen and proved. Cover loosely with oiled clingfilm/plastic wrap or a damp kitchen towel and leave to rise to the top of the pan for about 30 minutes, or until doubled in size. When risen, uncover and brush the tops with olive oil and lightly press in the chilli/chile rings. Scatter a few fennel seeds on top and bake the rolls for 35–45 minutes or until golden.

Meanwhile, make the basil and preserved lemon oil by putting the basil and oil into a blender and whizzing until smooth. Mix with the chopped preserved lemon, taste and season, and add vinegar if necessary.

When the buns are cooked, leave to cool in the pan if you want them very soft, or turn them out onto a wire rack to cool if you like them drier. Serve warm with the dipping oil.

PIZZETTE AND SMALL BITES

GOAT'S CHEESE AND PESTO PIZZETTE

Pizzette al caprino

½ recipe Basic Pizza Dough (page 12), making just 1 ball of dough

6 tablespoons Classic Pesto Genovese (page 20)

a small goat's cheese log with rind (300 g/10 oz.)

4 fat garlic cloves, thinly sliced

extra virgin olive oil, to glaze

sea salt and freshly ground black pepper

a round cookie cutter, 7 cm/3 inches (optional)

a baking sheet, lightly oiled

**MAKES 12 PIZZETTE
(7 CM/3 INCHES)**

Goat's cheese has become as fashionable in Italy as it is in Britain and the US. The variety to use is the one with a snowy white rind that will hold its shape in the oven – just cut the pizza bases to fit the sliced cheese. Coupled with freshly made pesto, this is a marriage made in heaven. The pizzette are perfect served with drinks, as they can be assembled ahead of time and cooked at the last moment. If you make them beforehand, prick the bases all over to prevent them from rising too much, add the toppings, then cover and refrigerate until ready to cook.

Preheat the oven to 220°C (425°F) Gas 7.

Uncover the dough, punch out the air and roll or pull very thinly on a well-floured surface. Using an upturned glass or a cookie cutter, stamp out twelve 7-cm/3-inch circles and lay on a lightly oiled baking sheet. Alternatively, cut the circles of dough to match the size of your goat cheese log. Spread the pizzette with a little pesto.

Slice the goat's cheese into 12 slices and lay a slice on top of the pesto. Arrange a couple of slices of garlic on the goat's cheese and brush with olive oil. Season and bake for 8–10 minutes or until the cheese is beginning to melt. Serve immediately.

'NDUJA AND BLACK OLIVE TAPENADE PIZZETTE

Pizzette con 'nduja e crema di olive nere

½ recipe Basic Pizza Dough (page 12), making just 1 ball of dough

1 small sweet red (bell) pepper

3 garlic cloves, skins on

2–3 tablespoons salted capers

225 g/8 oz. black wrinkly olives, stoned/pitted

12 boneless anchovy fillets

about 150 ml/⅔ cup mild olive oil

fresh lemon juice, to taste

45 ml/3 tablespoons chopped fresh parsley

250–300 g/9–10½ oz. 'nduja (spicy Calabrian sausage)

12 cherry tomatoes, halved

extra virgin olive oil, to glaze

fresh oregano, to garnish

sea salt and freshly ground black pepper

a round cookie cutter, 7 cm/3 inches (optional)

a baking sheet, lightly oiled

MAKES 12 PIZZETTE
(7 CM/3 INCHES)

The name 'tapenade' comes from the Provençal word *tapena* meaning 'capers' and is a thick sauce or spread made from capers, garlic and anchovies. This recipe adds rich dark olives and charred sweet (bell) pepper for a more intense, smoky flavour that is delicious with fiery 'nduja. Spread the rest on focaccia or add more oil for a dipping sauce.

Preheat the oven to 220°C (425°F) Gas 7.

First make the tapenade. Put the whole (bell) pepper and garlic cloves under a hot grill/broiler and grill/broil for about 15 minutes, turning until completely charred all over. Cool, rub off the skin (do not wash) and remove the stalk and seeds from the pepper. Peel the skin off the garlic. Rinse the capers and drain. Put all these in a food processor with the olives and anchovies and process until roughly chopped. With the motor running, slowly add the olive oil until you have a fairly smooth dark paste (process less if you prefer it rougher). Season with lemon juice and black pepper. Stir in the parsley. Store in a jar, covered with a layer of olive oil to exclude the air, for up to 1 month.

Uncover the dough, punch out the air and roll or pull very thinly on a well-floured surface. Using an upturned glass or a cookie cutter, stamp out twelve 7-cm/3-inch circles and lay on a lightly oiled baking sheet.

Spread the pizzette with a little black olive tapenade and top with a heaped teaspoon of 'nduja. Push in halved cherry tomatoes then brush with olive oil. Season if necessary and bake for 8–10 minutes. Serve immediately with oregano.

SARDENAIRA

25 g/1 cake compressed fresh yeast,
1 tablespoon/1 packet active dry yeast,
or 2 teaspoons fast-action dried yeast

½ teaspoon sugar

150 ml/⅔ cup warm milk

500 g/4¼ cups Italian '00' flour
or cake flour

100 ml/7 tablespoons extra virgin
olive oil

90 ml/6 tablespoons hand-hot water

2 onions, thinly sliced

1 kg/2¼ lb. fresh, very ripe tomatoes,
peeled and chopped, or 1 kg/2¼ lb.
(drained weight) canned whole
tomatoes

100 g/3½ oz. anchovies or sardines
in salt

12 or more whole garlic cloves,
unpeeled

100 g/3½ oz. or more small stoned/
pitted black Ligurian olives

1 tablespoon dried oregano

sea salt and freshly ground
black pepper

fresh oregano, to garnish

*a rectangular baking pan,
28 x 43 cm/11 x 15 inches and
approximately 2.5 cm/1 inch deep,
oiled*

SERVES 10

This amazingly savoury Ligurian focaccia is topped with a concentrated sauce of tomatoes, salted anchovies or salted sardines (hence the name) and whole melting cloves of garlic. It is perfect for outdoor eating, served in thin slices with a cold glass of wine or beer.

In a large bowl, cream the compressed yeast with the sugar and beat in the warm milk. Leave for 10 minutes until frothy. For other yeasts, follow the manufacturer's instructions.

Sift the flour with 1 teaspoon salt into a large bowl and make a well in the centre. Pour in the yeast mixture, 60 ml/4 tablespoons of the olive oil and the hand-hot water. Mix together with a round-bladed knife, then use your hands until the dough comes together. Tip out onto a lightly floured surface, wash and dry your hands, then knead briskly for 10–15 minutes until smooth, shiny and elastic. Try not to add any extra flour at this stage – a wetter dough is better. If you feel the dough is sticky, flour your hands and not the dough. The dough should be quite soft. If it is really too soft to handle, knead in a little more flour.

To test if the dough is ready, roll it into a fat sausage, take each end in either hand, lift the dough up and pull and stretch the dough outward, gently wiggling it up and down – it should stretch out quite easily. If it doesn't, it needs more kneading. Shape into a neat ball. Put it in an oiled bowl, cover with clingfilm/plastic wrap or a damp kitchen towel and let rise in a warm, draught-free place until doubled in size – about 1½ hours.

Heat the remaining olive oil in a large saucepan, add the onions and cook for about 10 minutes until beginning to soften and colour slightly. Add the tomatoes and cook gently until collapsed and very thick. Meanwhile, split the anchovies, remove the backbone, rinse and roughly chop. Stir into the sauce and season to taste.

Preheat the oven to 180°C (350°F) Gas 4. Knock back the dough, knead lightly, then stretch and pat it out into the prepared pan, pushing the dough well up the edges. Spread the sauce on top of the crust, cover with the whole garlic cloves and the olives, then sprinkle with the oregano. Drizzle with a little olive oil and bake for about 1 hour until the bread is golden. Serve sliced – hot, warm or cold, sprinkled with fresh oregano.

LITTLE FRIED NEAPOLITAN PIZZAS

Pizzelle aperte

These crisp little circles of fried pizza dough topped with a blob of tomato sauce, cool white mozzarella and fresh basil, are often served in bars with your aperitivi. Although best served straight from the pan, you can make the puffy pizza crusts beforehand, let them cool and store in an airtight container. To reheat, put them in a preheated oven at 180°C (350°F) Gas 4 for 2–3 minutes, then add the toppings and serve. A wok makes a perfect fryer for these.

½ recipe Basic Pizza Dough (page 12), making just 1 ball of dough

½ recipe Pizzaiola Sauce (page 19)

1 buffalo mozzarella, squeezed of excess water, then cut into tiny sticks

12 fresh basil leaves

vegetable or olive oil, for deep-frying

a round cookie cutter, 5 cm/2 inches (optional)

a wok or deep fat fryer

MAKES ABOUT 12 PIZZAS
(5 CM/2 INCHES)

Uncover the dough, punch out the air and roll or pull very thinly on a well-floured surface. Using an upturned glass or a cookie cutter, stamp out 12 or more 5-cm/2-inch circles.

Heat the oil in a wok or deep fat fryer to 190°C (375°F) or until a tiny piece of dough sizzles instantly when dropped in. Fry the pizzas, 4 at a time, for 2–3 minutes or until puffed and golden. You will have to turn them now and again so that they colour evenly. Remove with a slotted spoon and drain on paper towels.

Top with a little pizzaiola sauce, a stick of mozzarella and a basil leaf. Serve immediately while still hot.

LITTLE STUFFED FOCACCIA MUFFINS

Focaccette ripiene

½ recipe Deep-pan Focaccia (page 100), making just 1 ball of dough, risen twice but uncooked

8 tablespoons Classic Pesto Genovese (page 20)

24 small cherry tomatoes

1 cow's milk mozzarella (*fior di latte*), squeezed of excess water, then diced

sprigs of thyme or rosemary, to decorate

coarse sea salt

a round cookie cutter, 7 cm/3 inches (optional)

2 x 12-hole mini-muffin pans, oiled

MAKES ABOUT 24 MUFFINS

Almost like little muffins, these tiny treats hide a surprise when you bite into them – a tomato bathed in pesto and melting mozzarella. Make them in advance and reheat in a warm oven.

Preheat the oven to 200°C (400°F) Gas 6.

Uncover the dough, punch out the air and divide the dough into 4. Roll or pull each piece as thinly as you can on a well-floured work surface. Using an upturned glass or a cookie cutter, stamp out 6 little circles. Place a scant teaspoon of pesto in the middle of each circle, add a little mozzarella, then top with a cherry tomato. Bring the sides up and over the tomato and pinch to seal.

Put the muffins, sealed-side down, in the prepared mini-muffin pans. Brush the tops with olive oil, push in a herb sprig and sprinkle with salt.

Bake in the oven for 10–15 minutes until risen and cooked through. Tip out of the pans and eat warm, as a snack, with drinks.

Panzerotti

Panzerotti or 'little fat bellies' from the Italian pancia, meaning 'tummy,' are a great favourite in southern Italian pizzerias. The filling is usually some type of salami and cheese and they can be quite large. They puff up like swollen bellies when deep-fried.

½ recipe Basic Pizza Dough (page 12), making just 1 ball of dough

100 g/3½ oz. smoked mozzarella cheese, cut into small cubes

100g/3½ oz. *salame piccante* or chorizo, diced

200 g/¾ cup ricotta

60 g/⅔ cup freshly grated Parmesan cheese

3 tablespoons chopped fresh basil

vegetable or olive oil, for deep-frying

sea salt

a round cookie cutter, 7 cm/3 inches (optional)

a fluted cookie cutter, 7 cm/3 inches

a wok or deep fat fryer

MAKES ABOUT 15 PANZEROTTI

Mix together the mozzarella, salami, ricotta, Parmesan and basil. Season.

Uncover the dough, punch out the air and roll or pull very thinly. Using an upturned glass or a cookie cutter, stamp out about 15 little circles.

Place large spoonfuls of the filling onto one half of each dough circle. Fold the other half over, pinching well to seal, then neaten the edges with a fluted cookie cutter.

Heat the oil to 190°C (375°F) Gas 5 in the wok or deep fat fryer and deep-fry the panzerotti in batches until puffed, crisp and brown. Flip them over to cook both sides evenly. Drain on paper towels and season with salt. Serve immediately while still warm and gooey.

CRISPY PIZZA SHEETS
Pizza croccante

1 recipe Basic Pizza Dough (page 12) or any leftover dough

2 teaspoons dried rosemary (optional)

extra virgin olive oil, to glaze

coarse sea salt

2 large, heavy baking sheets, lightly oiled

**MAKES ABOUT
6 LARGE SHEETS**

I bought a factory-produced version of this in Tuscany and it inspired me to bake my own. It's so easy to make that you quickly get into the rhythm of preparing it until it becomes second nature.

Preheat the oven to 230°C (450°F) Gas 8, or as hot as you can.

Uncover the dough, punch out the air and knead in the dried rosemary (if using). Divide the dough into 6 and roll or pull it directly onto the prepared baking sheets. Press it out with your fingers as large and flat as you can. The dough should be so thin you can almost see through it – and it doesn't have to be even. Brush it lightly with olive oil and scatter with salt. Bake for about 8 minutes until golden, lightly bubbled, dry and crisp. Shatter the sheets like poppadoms to serve.

'ROOF TILES'
Ciappe

1 tablespoon sea salt

100 ml/⅓ cup warm water

250 g/1¼ cups Italian '0' or '00' flour, or unbleached plain/all-purpose flour

2 tablespoons extra virgin olive oil

2 large, heavy baking sheets

MAKES 8–10 TILES

In Ligurian dialect, a *ciappa* is a thin, flat stone that has been used for baking flatbreads since the dawn of time but can also mean a slate roof tile. Nowadays these stones are used to cook meat and fish at the table.

Mix the salt with the warm water until dissolved. Sift the flour into a medium bowl and make a well in the centre. Pour in the salty water and olive oil. Mix well, then knead the dough lightly for a couple of minutes until it is smooth. The dough should be firmer than that of pizza. Wrap it in clingfilm/plastic wrap and let rest for 15 minutes.

Preheat the oven to 180°C (350°F) Gas 4.

Divide the dough into 8–10 pieces. Roll or pull each piece into a long oval. Roll them as thinly as you can and keep the work surface well floured to prevent sticking. Alternatively you can use a pasta machine to roll them out if you are making a large quantity.

Lay the tiles on the baking sheets and prick all over with a fork with large tines. Make sure they are liberally peppered with holes. Bake in the oven for 15–20 minutes or until evenly pale golden and dried out. Let cool on a wire rack and store in an airtight container for up to 2 weeks.

ANCHOVY TWISTS
Ficattole

½ recipe Basic Pizza Dough (page 12), making just 1 ball of dough

50 g/1¾ oz. canned anchovies in oil, drained and chopped

vegetable or olive oil, for deep-frying

sea salt and freshly ground black pepper

a wok or deep fat fryer

MAKES 15–20 TWISTS

For all you anchovy-lovers out there, these fit the bill. Transform leftover pizza dough (or use fresh dough) by flavouring it with anchovies. The combination of these simple anchovy twists and a glass of chilled white wine truly transports you to a sunny terrace in southern Italy.

Uncover the dough, punch out the air and knead in the anchovies. Roll or pull thinly and cut into long rectangles with a crinkled pastry wheel or a sharp knife. Make a slash in the middle of each rectangle, bring one end up and push through the slit, pulling it through loosely to make a roughly twisted shape.

Heat the oil in the wok or deep fat fryer to 190°C (375°F) Gas 5 and fry the twists in batches until golden and crisp. Drain well on paper towels, then sprinkle with salt and freshly ground black pepper. Serve warm. You can store these in an airtight container and reheat them for a couple of minutes in a warm oven when you are ready to serve them.

PEPPERED BREADSTICKS

Grissini pepato

We all know the paper packets containing a couple of breadsticks which many Italian restaurants serve, but these are a more sophisticated version and can be made using leftover pizza dough. Just knead in the black pepper or any other flavouring that suits your fancy.

½ recipe Basic Pizza Dough (page 12), making just 1 ball of dough

2 tablespoons cracked black pepper

2 tablespoons extra virgin olive oil

25 g/2 tablespoons butter, melted

**MAKES ABOUT
20 BREADSTICKS**

Make the pizza dough according to the recipe on page 12, adding the cracked pepper to the ingredients. Mix the olive oil and melted butter together. Before the first rising, roll or pull the dough into a thin rectangle, brush all over with the olive oil and butter mixture and roll up loosely like a jelly roll. Flatten with the palm of your hand, then lift it onto a floured work surface, cover with clingfilm/plastic wrap and let rise for 30 minutes.

Preheat the oven to 200°C (400°F) Gas 6.

Flatten the risen dough with your hand again to knock out the air then roll out to a thickness of 5 mm/¼ inch. Cut into long, thin strips and twist. Lay these onto a baking sheet and mist with water. Bake for 5 minutes, mist again, then bake for a further 10–15 minutes until golden and crisp. Keep an eye on them while they are baking as they can burn.

PARMESAN FRITTERS
Chizze

Here's another quick snack made from leftover pizza dough and often served in bars. All you need is some fresh Parmesan cheese and you've got a delicious appetite-whetter. Just don't eat too many!

½ recipe Basic Pizza Dough
(page 12) or Sicilian Pizza Dough
(page 16), making just 1 ball of dough

50 g/½ cup freshly grated Parmesan
cheese, plus extra to dust

vegetable or olive oil, for deep-frying

a round cookie cutter (optional)

a wok or deep fat fryer

MAKES ABOUT 16 FRITTERS

Uncover the dough, punch out the air and roll or pull as thinly as you can, flouring the surface well. Using an upturned glass or a cookie cutter, stamp out as many circles as you can – you can make them any size. Place a little mound of Parmesan in the centre of each one and fold in half, pinching the edges together.

Heat the oil in the wok or deep fat fryer to 190°C (375°F) Gas 5. A piece of stale bread dropped in should sizzle and turn golden in a few seconds. Fry in batches until puffed and golden on both sides. Drain well on paper towels, then toss the fritters in some grated Parmesan. Serve hot.

PANCETTA AND FENNEL PUFFS

Coccoli

200 ml/¾ cup milk

50 g/2 oz. pure lard, roughly chopped

37 g/1½ cakes compressed fresh yeast
or 1 packet fast-action dried yeast

400 g/3½ cups Italian '0' or '00' flour,
or unbleached all-purpose flour

50 g/2 oz. pancetta, finely diced

1 teaspoon fennel seeds,
lightly crushed

vegetable or olive oil, for deep-frying

sea salt

a wok or deep-fat fryer

MAKES ABOUT 30–40 PUFFS

These *coccoli* ('little darlings!') are a type of savoury doughnut or *bomboloni* flavoured with pancetta. I add lightly crushed fennel seeds, a flavouring that is very popular in Tuscany, especially with cured pork. They are deep-fried until crisp on the outside and soft inside and can be kept warm in the oven. Make sure they are piping hot and sprinkled liberally with sea salt when you serve them. Grind fennel seeds over them for a special finishing touch. These are especially wonderful if you have the chance to fry them in pure olive oil. The dough can also be rolled out thinly and cut into squares, then fried.

Put the milk and lard in a saucepan and heat gently until the lard has melted. Don't let the milk get too hot. Crumble in the compressed yeast (if using) and beat until dissolved. Sift the flour and a good pinch of salt into a bowl and make a well in the centre. If you are using fast-action yeast, stir it into the flour now. Pour in the warm milk mixture and add the pancetta and fennel seeds. Mix to a soft dough, adding more flour, if necessary. Form into a ball, cover with clingfilm/plastic wrap or a damp kitchen towel and let rise for 2 hours or until doubled in size.

Heat the oil in a wok or deep fat fryer to 180°C (350°F). A piece of stale bread dropped in should sizzle and turn golden in a few seconds.

Uncover the dough, punch out the air and knead for 1 minute. Pull off small walnut-sized pieces of dough, about 2 cm/¾ inch and roll into rough balls. Fry in batches for about 2–3 minutes until pale brown and puffy. Drain well and tip onto paper towels. Sprinkle with salt and serve while still hot.

RESOURCES

Pizza and Italian food

Vera Pizza Napoletana
www.pizzanapoletana.org
The Italian specifications of true Neapolitan pizza. Training and restaurant certification for persons and restaurant-owners interested in making and/or offering authentic Neapolitan pizza as established by the guidelines of the Verace Pizza Napoletana Association, founded in Naples.

Baroni
www.baronialimentari.com
Mercato Centrale, Florence, Italy
The Baroni family offers top-quality condiments, oils, aged balsamic vinegars, fresh Alpine butter, fresh black and white truffles in season and truffle products, and will ship them all over the world.

Bartolini
www.bartolinifirenze.it
Via dei Servi, 30, Florence, Italy
Italian cookware shop and general temple of gastronomy.

Caputo
www.mulinocaputo.it
'Flour of Naples', this producer offers Italian '0' and '00' flours from which to make pizza dough.

Forno Bravo®
www.fornobravo.com
Sells outdoor and indoor pizza ovens, equipment and offers advice on how to use them.

Gambero Rosso®
www.gamberorosso.it
Fascinating Italian gastronomic website with information on books, food and wine, etc.

Italian Made
www.italianmade.com
Very interesting official site for the foods and wines of Italy. Includes how to eat Italian-style, where to eat and buy Italian produce, and the history and lore of Italian foods.

Seeds of Italy
www.seedsofitaly.com
Real Italian seeds supplied for UK mail-order for growing your own Italian fruit, vegetables and herbs, plus olive oils and seasonings.

Seeds from Italy
www.growitalian.com
Real Italian seeds supplied for US mail-order.

Slow Food®
www.slowfood.com
An international association that promotes food and wine culture, and defends agricultural bio-diversity worldwide, protects cultural identities tied to food and gastronomic traditions and safeguards food cultivation and inherited processing techniques.

Other useful resources

UK
Borough Market
www.boroughmarket.org.uk
London's most renowned food market.

Carluccio's
www.carluccios.com
Owned by well-known gastronome, Antonio Carluccio, these Italian delicatessens and restaurants stock a wide array of Italian ingredients including spicy Calabrian sausage 'nduja.

Nife is Life
www.nifeislife.com
Premium Italian ingredients available to order online for delivery across the UK.

Orchard Ovens
www.orchardwoodovens.co.uk
The UK's sole importer and distributor of renowned Valoriani wood-burning ovens for the garden or kitchen, made in Reggello, near Florence, Italy.

Sous Chef
www.souschef.co.uk
Fantastic source of quality ingredients (including 'nduja) and cooking equipment.

US

'Nduja Artisans
www.ndujaartisans.com
Stockist listings for specialist Italian ingredients, including 'nduja.

ChefShop.com
www.chefshop.com
Seattle-based website offering a seasonal selection of more than 1,000 of the very best artisan-produced foods and fresh products from around the world. A broad selection of domestic and imported olive oils, balsamic vinegars, exotic and hard-to-find spices and herbs, and seasonal Parmigiano-Reggiano cheeses from Italy.

Crate & Barrel
www.crateandbarrel.com
Fantastic source of housewares and kitchen accessories, as well as gourmet foods like quality olive oil and pizza sauce.

Dean & DeLuca
www.deandeluca.com
High-quality food and kitchenware.

Eataly
www.eataly.com
A large Italian marketplace with locations in New York, Chicago and London, UK. Offers a variety of restaurants, food and beverage counters, bakery, retail items and a cooking school.

igourmet.com
www.igourmet.com
Refrigerated deliveries of perishable specialist goods including burrata cheese.

King Arthur Flour
www.kingarthurflour.com
Vermont's venerable milling company is an invaluable resource for serious pizza-makers and bread-bakers. Stocking every flour imaginable, including Italian-style, spelt, buckwheat, triticale flours, plus malt products and countless other baking aids and gourmet food supplies.

Penzeys
www.penzeys.com
Penzeys Spices offers more than 250 herbs, spices and seasonings, including blue poppy seeds, white, green or pink peppercorns, white and green cardamom and premium saffron.

Williams-Sonoma
www.williams-sonoma.com
Online cookshop with everything for home-baking and cooking, including round and square baking stones, wooden pizza peels and Bialetti pizza cutters.

Zingermans
www.zingermans.com
Zingerman's selection of cheeses, estate-bottled olive oils and varietal vinegars is unmatched. Their website is packed with information.

PICTURE CREDITS

INDEX

PRACTICAL PRINCESS
PERFECT WARDROBE

Declutter and re-jig your
closet to transform your life

ELIKA GIBBS

RYLAND PETERS & SMALL
LONDON • NEW YORK

Senior designer: Sonya Nathoo
Senior editor: Annabel Morgan
Picture research: Emily Westlake
Production: Patricia Harrington
Art director: Leslie Harrington
Publishing director: Alison Starling

First published in 2011.
This revised edition published in 2019
by Ryland Peters & Small
20–21 Jockey's Fields, London WC1R 4BW
341 East 116th Street, New York NY 10029

www.rylandpeters.com

10 9 8 7 6 5 4 3 2 1

A CIP record for this book is available from the
British Library.

Library of Congress cataloging-in-publication data has
been applied for

ISBN: 978-1-78879-070-3

Printed in China

the shop at bluebird
350 KINGS ROAD LONDON
SW3 5UU   020 7351 3873
THESHOPATBLUEBIRD.COM

contents

introduction

The following pages contain the tried-and-tested Practical Princess formula that I use at work every day. I work with a myriad of clients whose individual needs are many and varied, and so I tailor each job slightly to benefit them. Some clients will only require wardrobe organization, while others need to go through the full process of assessment, organization and shopping.

I do not claim to be a fashionista in any way, shape or form, but I have had the privilege to work with many fashion icons. My unique formula has worked for each and every one of them, as they have been able to get clarity in their vast wardrobes.

By following these steps, I hope that you too will achieve 'closet clarity' and enjoy getting dressed again.

the practical princess story

Practical Princess evolved and grew without me actually even knowing it. It didn't begin in the conventional way that a lot of companies do. I didn't have a vision, and certainly didn't have a business plan, but this is the story of how it all started.

In my late twenties, I opened up a designer and couture evening dress hire shop in Knightsbridge, London, with my then business partner Arabella Bodie. Our aim was to have a shop where you could hire a beautiful long gown for the night without having to spend thousands of pounds buying a dress you might only wear once. We stocked gorgeous dresses from designers such as Bruce Oldfield, Amanda Wakeley, Jenny Packham and Vera Wang. Ladies could also hire jewellery, shoes, handbags and pashminas, making it a one-stop shop.

We also sold the original 'Magic Knickers'. These had not yet hit the market – Arabella and I had sourced them from a European trade fair – and they became a great hit. They were so popular that at times we would sit up all night packing hundreds of pairs of knickers to send out worldwide.

After running the shop for a number of years, our lives started to change. Arabella got married and – whoops! – I got pregnant. Becoming a single mum and Arabella leaving Bodie & Gibbs had a dramatic effect upon my life. Financially, with a baby to support, I was finding it hard to survive on the salary that I drew. I had to find a way to earn more money.

Whether by luck, fate or perfect timing, I was asked by a successful and busy executive to help organize and restructure her household. I was hesitant about accepting the offer, as I had no training or qualifications in this field, but I was assured that I could do it and I really needed the extra cash. Although I was still running the shop, during the next couple of years I spent a day a week reorganizing every nook and cranny of her home, from kitchen cupboards to wardrobes. I also helped hire and train her staff, and shopped for anything from bed linens to new pairs of jeans. You name it, I did it!

At this point my main focus was still Bodie & Gibbs. Over the years, I had built some wonderful relationships with a number of clients who I would regularly dress for parties and events. I have always been one to push the boundaries, and I had encouraged many of them to move out of their comfort zone and try something different. I was flattered when they started to ask me to help them with their day-to-day look too, and this was how I started personal shopping.

Not all personal shoppers will look at a client's wardrobe before they shop, but for me it was a logical step, so that I could see what clothes they had and what was missing. I was often shocked to discover the way in which these ladies kept their clothes. No wonder they couldn't get dressed! I realized that these women were not the unstylish, hopeless cases that they thought.

In fact, some had wonderful pieces lurking in the depths of their wardrobe but that were just not getting used.

I realized that I couldn't help my clients or take them shopping until I could get 'closet clarity'. And this is where my formula began to develop. I didn't want to humiliate or embarrass anyone, but I needed them to try on their clothes so that we could establish what worked and what didn't. By rehanging and reorganizing their closets, we were able to establish the gaps that needed to be filled when we went shopping.

I guess that this is when Practical Princess started to take form. It slowly evolved and grew by word of mouth, and bookings began to include household and office moves. Thankfully, all the knowledge and know-how I had obtained from running my shop, along with the new experiences gained from different clients' needs, helped me to take on these new challenges. Fearful as I was to take the next step, as my livelihood and that of my little girl depended upon it, I decided to close the door on my dress shop and concentrate on making Practical Princess my full-time profession.

That was five years ago, and even though there have been trials and tribulations, tears and laughter, my business has expanded and I now have 'princesses' who run their own teams. I have developed my own product range and opened a storage centre for my clients to store off-season and archive clothes.

On reflection, I wonder whether I would have had the foresight and courage to start Practical Princess if I had not been in dire straits. I certainly felt the fear, but I didn't have the time to think about the consequences if things went wrong, and for that I am grateful.

I now consider myself so lucky to love what I do for a living. The variety and challenges that face me day to day are never boring, and I have met some amazing people along the way who have been instrumental in supporting me. New opportunities and ventures are again being placed in front of me – this book being one. The fear came back, but it was a challenge I couldn't resist!

wardrobe assessment

does your wardrobe reflect your life?

The Practical Princess process always starts the same way, with a consultation to meet my client face to face in their own environment. This is to help me build a picture of the client, so that when I look through their wardrobe I can see whether their clothes reflect their lifestyle. I ask my clients to tell me a bit about themselves while I gently question them to get the answers I need. I want you to ask yourself the same questions:

- Do you work?
- How do you spend your days?
- What's your marital status?
- Are you a parent?
- What's your social life?
- Do you have any upcoming events?
- What are your interests?
- Do you travel?
- Are you happy with your weight and well-being?
- Have you had any life-changing events/circumstances?
- Where do you live and what's the climate?

By answering these questions you should be able to see whether your wardrobe reflects your lifestyle. Let me give you an example, but don't try and identify with the character, as this is purely to illustrate why this process is vital.

One of my clients is a forty-something female, divorced from a wealthy banker and with no children. She was having a crisis. Her old life required her to wear dresses and suits that, she said, 'made her feel like the mother of the bride'. However, her life had dramatically changed. She was about to embark on a new career where the dress code boundary was blurred. Having been single

for a few years, she had developed a crush on a younger man and desperately
wanted to become a cougar! Her holidays were always spent with her family,
who still expected her to conform, and her self-worth was on the floor. She
was in desperate need of help. She felt she had no sense of style, no longer
knew who she was and was struggling to get dressed in the morning.

When I looked through her wardrobe, I could see that her old and new lives
were all tangled up. There was the normal wardrobe chaos that I always see,
but from a psychological point of view she had not yet let go of her old life.

By going through her wardrobe garment by garment, she began to see that
more than half her clothes were no longer relevant to her life. A smile finally
spread over her face as she realized that it was not because she had no style,
but because she had changed as a woman. This gave her the encouragement
she needed to continue with my process. What people don't seem to realize
is that their clothes can tie them to an identity that is stuck in the past.

trying on

A proper assessment takes longer than expected, so don't dive in hoping to sort out your wardrobe in a couple of hours on a Saturday morning. You either need to set aside a proper chunk of time – such as a whole weekend – or break the tasks down into bite-size pieces by doing all your skirts one evening, all your trousers another.

STEP BY STEP

I don't want you to try all of your clothes on just as they come out of your wardrobe – this will quickly become overwhelming and you may just give up! I find that if I stick with one garment type at a time, it keeps my clients focused and the process is much more successful. The repetition of trying on the same item of clothing over and over allows them to make a good comparison of style and fit. This gives my clients the confidence and ability to continue the process later on their own. If you do the same, it will be easier for you to gauge what to get rid of and what to keep.

Breaking clothes down into sub-sections will help you even more. Let me give you an example: if you are working on trousers, put them into categories – jeans, combats, tailored trousers and so on – as this will give you an idea of how many similar pairs you have and which is the better fit.

If you find that you have, say, five pairs of black trousers, are there some that you have not worn for a while or perhaps never wear? A lot of my clients hang onto trousers because they think that they are timeless. Yet trousers seem to date quicker than anything else. This is why it is so important to try everything on and take the time to look at yourself properly in a full-length mirror.

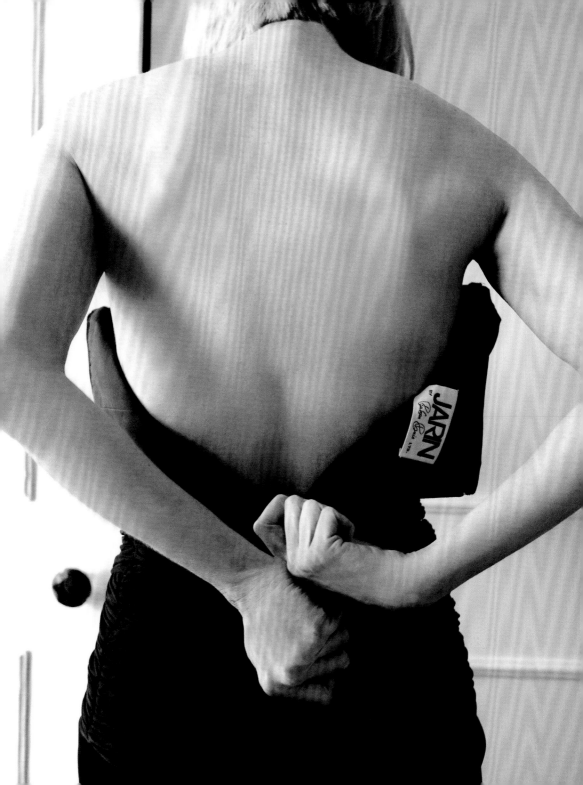

the six-pile process

As you try on your clothes, you will need to create six piles to help you keep order throughout the process. I often use sticky notes to mark my piles, so that items don't get mixed up.

1 KEEP
The fit and the look are working for you.
There must be no question mark hanging over these items. They must look good, fit well and be in good condition. They must also be relevant to your lifestyle, as identified in your wardrobe assessment. At the end of this exercise, don't panic if this is your smallest pile. You haven't gone wrong; you are simply being realistic about what does and doesn't look good. You must trust in this process, or you will not benefit from my tried-and-tested formula.

2 ARCHIVE
Pieces that you no longer wear, but don't want to part with.
Of course, there are always pieces that we want to hang onto, and archiving clothes allows us to return to and reuse things at a later date. I have kept some cherished pieces that I can no longer wear for my little girl. You may also have items that you want to hand down to someone special. Having said all of this, you still have to be realistic about how much you keep and where you are going to store it. If you are not wearing it, you shouldn't see it!

3 MAYBE
Your headache pile: should it stay or should it go?
When you are umming and ahhing over an item, there are a few important things to consider. Does it fit? Is it flattering? Is the cut, shape or detail dated? For instance, even if you don't have a good pair of jeans to put in your KEEP pile, don't be scared to get rid of unflattering pairs. It is better to have a gap in your wardrobe that you can fill when you go shopping. This will help you to buy what you need and stop impulse buying. When the gaps are identified, you strip away the illusion of having a complete wardrobe with loads of clothes yet nothing to wear. Does this sound familiar?

4 EDIT

Things to move on, including mistakes, wrong sizes or worn-out items.
The key to editing successfully is brutal honesty. We have all made a fashion
faux pas (or two) and later destroyed the photographic evidence. With
hindsight, remortgaging the house to buy that fabulous dress was clearly a
mistake! Just because something is designer or expensive doesn't give it
the privilege to sit in your wardrobe. This pile should also contain clothes that
are tired, worn out or over-laundered. There's nothing worse than a dingy
off-white vest, even if it is one of your day-to-day basic pieces that you might
be reluctant to throw away. These wardrobe basics need to be continually
edited and replaced.

5 DRY-CLEANING, LAUNDRY AND ALTERATIONS

Very Important!
There is nothing worse than going to put something on only to find it needs to
be dry-cleaned or laundered. Equally annoying is when you have planned an

outfit and then realize that a zip is broken or a seam has come undone. Make sure that your clothes are always ready to wear. Don't put dirty or damaged pieces into your wardrobe until they have been dealt with.

Often, dated clothes can be modernized with a simple alteration. It is amazing what a difference simply changing a hemline or swapping the buttons can make to an outfit. So put items that can be updated on this pile.

6 SEASONAL CHANGEOVER

The clothes that you wear in the depth of winter or the height of summer should be packed away for the reverse season. Doing this will create space in your wardrobe and help you identify any gaps.

The six-pile process may seem over the top and a waste of time, but if you stick to this tried-and-tested formula, I promise the benefits will be endless.

what to do with your edit pile

CAR BOOT/YARD SALE

This is probably my favourite way of moving on my edit pile as well as any unwanted household and family items. Not everyone may relish getting up at the crack of dawn to sell their unwanted possessions, but personally I get a real buzz from them! By trial and error I have honed my sales technique. I did no preparation at all for my first sale and started off with plastic bags full of clothes and a trestle table. Of course I ended up in chaos, underselling a lot of my items, as I could not display them adequately. I learned from this experience and realized that I needed to put into practice the basic formula I use at work. As ever, organization is the key.

The next time, I put prime items onto hangers and placed bags, shoes and toys in plastic tubs. I knew this would help me set up my stall quickly and efficiently. The effect that I wanted this time was not that of a jumble sale but a well-arranged, enticing stall, giving me a platform to sell more and in turn make more cash. I am happy to report that this time I was successful!

Here are some tools and tips that helped me:
- Hangers (this is the *only* time that wire ones are allowed!)
- Hanging rail
- Trestle/wallpaper table
- Baskets, boxes, plastic tubs
- Plastic bags for sold items
- Money belt (stocked with plenty of change)
- Plastic sheeting to cover your items in case it rains
- A friend to give you moral support
- Wear layered clothing, as the early mornings can be cold
- Tidy up your stall in the quiet periods
- Be realistic with pricing – you are there to sell, not to bring things back home
- Don't bring unsold items back into the house – take them straight to the local charity shop/thrift store

EBAY

Pretty much anything can be sold on eBay, due to its huge global audience. For some people it is easy and very profitable, but for others it is time-consuming with little reward.

Each item you want to sell has to be photographed in several different ways, showing as much detail as possible. A written description is also required, providing measurements and any other relevant details. The more information you give, the less time you will need to spend answering buyer's enquiries.

Ebay have strict rules and regulations to protect their buyers and only give you five working days to ship the goods after payment is received. Send parcels and packages by recorded mail, as your item will then be insured and can be tracked.

I am hopeless at the eBay process because I don't have the time or patience needed. However, I do recognize eBay's selling potential, so my company, Practical Princess, uses it to sell designer pieces that clients no longer want.

RESALE SHOPS

There are more and more resale shops cropping up all over the place. It is important to do your research before you choose a shop, as they all have different criteria. Here are some questions you should ask:
• Do they only take designer labels?
• Do the clothes have to be dry-cleaned and in impeccable condition?
• What percentage do they take from the selling price?
• Do they take off-season clothes?
• How long after an item is sold are you paid? And what form does payment take?
• What happens to any unsold items?

CHARITY/THRIFT STORES

If you can afford to, or have a heart of gold, the best way to get rid of your edit pile is to give it to charity.

The easiest route is a quick drop at your local charity shop/thrift store. If you can't find one that supports your favourite charity, you could do the same as some of my clients. They sell their clothes through resale or eBay then donate the proceeds to their chosen cause.

If you can afford to, or have a heart of gold, the best way to get rid of your edit pile is to give it to charity.

what to do with your unwanted clothes

	PROS	CONS
CAR BOOT/ YARD SALE	• All the profit is yours • Likely to sell all unwanted items • You get some fresh air	• Haggling with punters over small change will drive you mad • Might not get as much money as you hoped per item. • Early start!
RESALE SHOP	• Little effort required • Competitively priced	• 40–60% commission charged • Off-season garments not always taken • Labels are selected at shop's discretion
EBAY	• Worldwide audience • Can get people bidding up on items	• Time-consuming, in all aspects: photographing, corresponding with bidders, packaging & posting and returns • Fees • Unless you have a minimum reserve price, you could end up with pennies • Getting your ratings up so that people trust you takes time
CHARITY/ THRIFT STORE	• Recycling • Helping others • Everything taken	• Getting it there • It is unhelpful and in some places illegal to leave donations outside the shop (out of hours)

storage

In my late teens and early twenties I moved from flat to flat, not caring or worrying about how my clothes were packed or stored. I was forever giving my parents boxes and cases of things I wanted them to keep for me. When I eventually opened them years later, it was soul-destroying to see the damage that damp and moths had caused. I wish I had known then what I know now – how a few simple steps could have saved my clothes.

Most of the time we have little choice as to where we store our archive, but it is imperative that we choose a damp- and sunlight-free zone. Any places that suffer from extreme temperature swings should be avoided, as should badly ventilated or uninsulated attics, basements and garages.

Your storage space will determine what you store your clothes in. Most of us have to store items in boxes or suitcases, since it is rare to find spare hanging space. It is preferable to use specialized cardboard dress boxes because they are not completely airtight, enabling the garments to breathe. It is also very important that you launder or dry-clean all clothes before they are stored. If something has been worn, even if it looks and smells clean, there will be skin cells and sweat left on the garment that will inevitably attract moths.

Before you start packing, wash your hands so that you do not transfer skin oils onto the clothes. Line the box with acid-free tissue paper. The trick is to make sure that you lay or fold each garment properly. The fewer folds you make, the better. Creases can become permanent on certain fabrics, and this should be avoided at all costs.

Each garment will require different care. Wedding dresses, ball gowns and other special items will need their own boxes and extra care should be taken when packing them. Acid-free tissue paper should be interleaved between folds, and crumpled tissue paper used to stuff the sleeves and bodice.

This will help to keep the shape, prevent creasing and ensure the longevity of your garments. If you are packing a number of items in one box, the same principle applies: interleave each garment when folding and use extra sheets of tissue paper to separate them. Some fabrics, trimmings and buttons may need to be treated differently. Metal buttons should be wrapped in acid-free tissue paper or even removed, as they can corrode and leave a nasty stain on fabric. When storing shoes, bags and accessories, make sure that you use acid-free tissue paper to wrap and stuff the bags.

If you are going to hang stored clothes, it is best to use breathable hanging garment bags. I use these in my storage centre for clients who do not have enough space to archive all their clothes. They protect garments from rubbing against one another or snagging. The bags are wide and long enough to prevent creasing, and a little space is left between each garment so that they are not all jammed together.

A moth deterrent must be placed in each box or bag. Slip this in between the sheets of tissue paper to avoid contact with the garments. They must be changed regularly, on average every three to six months. Replacing the moth repellent gives you a chance to check that the clothes are still in good condition.

CATALOGUING

I recommend that you photograph any item that you are storing for a long period of time. I photograph each garment on a mannequin and insert the picture in the dress bag pocket. When storing items in boxes, I create a written and photographic inventory of what's inside. This may seem unnecessary, but it is surprising how quickly we forget what we have packed away. It also makes it quick and easy to locate an item when it is needed.

SHORT-TERM STORAGE

I prefer to have only the current season's clothes hanging in a wardrobe. Of course, this is dependent on space, but if you can separate your summer and winter clothes, you will find it a lot easier to get dressed (note that I have not mentioned spring or autumn clothes, as these are usually transitional pieces that will carry us into the next season).

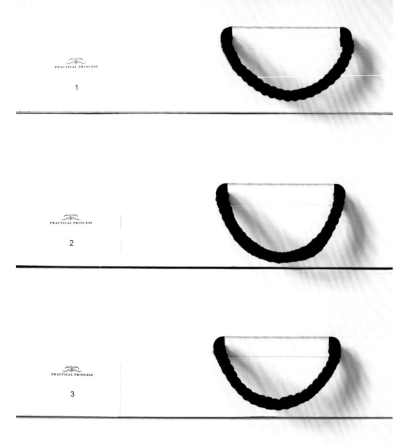

What to put away at the end of each season:

• Heavy winter coats. Shoulder covers will protect them against dust, saving on dry-cleaning bills.

• Pack up your resort wear, as you will only be wearing it on holiday. You don't want kaftans and sun hats mixed up with your day-to-day wear.

• Ski wear can be put into vacuum bags. This is not my favourite way of storing clothes, but it is extremely economical on space.

• Knits that you won't be wearing until next season can be stored in a variety of ways: plastic boxes, vacuum bags and sweater bags, or simply folded and piled on a high shelf at the top of your wardrobe.

• Note that if you are using vacuum bags for storage, steaming will be necessary before you use them again.

the cataloguing process

Red-carpet moments, gala balls and charity events all require dresses that scream drama. Unfortunately, they have a very short lifespan.

Clients of mine who are in the public eye tend not to be able to wear these dresses more than a few times, as they are constantly photographed. For these clients we create garment catalogues with several purposes. They are either to provide an archive record, for insurance purposes or for people with multiple homes, so that items are quick to locate should they need them.

Christian Dior	Derek Lam	DVF	DVF
Gucci	Julien MacDonald	Kaat Tilley	Luca Luca

Marchesa Notte

Matthew Williamson

Oscar de la Renta

Reem Acra

Reem Acra

Reem Acra

Reem Acra

RM

Roberto Cavalli

Stella McCartney

Valentino

Victoria Beckham

organizing
your wardrobe

adapting your space

Space seems to be a recurring issue in my line of work. No matter how large or how many cupboards somebody has, there never seems to be enough room. On quite a few occasions I have had to remind clients that I am the Practical Princess and not the fairy godmother, as it was physically impossible to fit all their clothes into the space available. I would love to have a magic wand, but unfortunately I don't! The only powers I might have are those obtained through experience and knowing how to maximize and use space to its best advantage.

Structurally, there will be elements in your wardrobe, cupboards or walk-in closet that you cannot move or alter. However, hanging rails can usually be repositioned and this will help you optimize your space and ensure that items have enough length to hang without getting crumpled.

Adjusting your hanging rails will give you a hanging length that suits your needs. Fitting two rails at different heights above one another in your wardrobe is another way to maximize your space. This is good for shorter items such as jackets, skirts and trousers and tops.

The pictures here and on the previous pages demonstrate how existing wardrobe space can easily be adapted. A shelf has been removed from this wardrobe and the hanging rail has been moved up to allow for an extra rail to be added below. This simple adjustment instantly doubles the wardrobe capacity and is ideal if you have lots of shorter items to hang. The beauty of this method is that it is not permanent, and if you wish to revert to the original configuration, the changes are easily reversible (don't chuck away the shelf).

If your cupboards are particularly wide or deep, double hanging rails one behind the other could be a consideration. However, you have to make sure that two hangers can sit side by side and fit comfortably in the wardrobe space so that your clothes will not be crushed.

Slanted wall hooks can be handy for hanging items in cupboards that are very shallow. Hidden dead space or small alcoves are also great places to fit these hooks if you have limited hanging space elsewhere.

Shelving is usually an inexpensive way of creating more space, and it is great for storing handbags, shoes, sweaters and so on. Extra shelves can often be added to existing wardrobes or cupboards, optimizing your storage space further.

If you don't have drawers inside your wardrobe, a free-standing drawer unit is a must. There are certain items that just have to live in a drawer, such as underwear, socks and sleepwear. And so many other items also benefit from being housed in a drawer, including T-shirts, clutch bags, gloves, belts, sunglasses… the list goes on and on.

WALK-IN WARDROBES

It is surprising how cheaply and easily one can make a walk-in closet out of a small spare room and easily be able to convert it back. By fixing rails onto the walls and/or using free-standing garment rails, a walk-in wardrobe-cum-dressing room will start to take shape. Extra storage such as shelving, trunks and chests of drawers can be added.

If you happen to be having built-in wardrobes fitted or making a permanent walk-in, here are a few tips to help you with your plan:

• Shelves should be movable. Make as many peg holes as possible, preferably every 10mm/½inch so that shelf heights can easily be adjusted. Make extra shelves, as you may need them.

• There are two ways to attach hanging rails: either beneath a shelf or directly to the sides of the wardrobe. It is essential that these are also adjustable.

• Measure the drop of your rehung clothes so that you know the width and height of hanging space you will need.

• Think about your drawer size and what you need to store in them. Drawers that are too deep can be counterproductive, because things can be lost and forgotten at the bottom.

• Think about the wardrobe doors. Sliding doors are space-saving, but they could stop you from viewing your clothes as a whole.

cleaning your space

When was the last time you took everything out of your wardrobe and gave it a really good clean? Go to your wardrobe, push your clothes to one side and run your finger along the hanging rail. It is more than likely that your fingertip will be covered in dust. Don't be horrified – you are not alone! I don't know why, but people rarely clean inside their wardrobes. We wouldn't eat off a dirty plate, so why would we hang clean clothes in a dusty wardrobe? You might not end up with food poisoning, but dust is made up partly from old skin cells – yuk!

When dust builds up it has a horrible stale smell and, before you know it, this will be impregnated into your clothes. Unfortunately, we get used to familiar smells around us and might not even notice this. I am not saying that your clothes smell, but it is worth keeping this in mind.

If there is a slight dusty smell, lemons cut in half, gently squeezed, covered with muslin and tied at the bottom will help to eradicate any unpleasant odours. The other trick is to use bowls of steaming water infused with an essence such as rose. Both of these solutions should be placed at the bottom of the wardrobe and changed when the water cools or the lemon becomes dry. Keep the wardrobe door closed and be careful that no item touches either of them.

I have used the boiling water tip for clothes that have been stored badly and had a particularly musty smell. I once made a mini-steam room in a small bathroom by filling the bath and sink with boiling water and essence to create a sauna-like effect. The clothes were hung on a hanging rail with spaces in between them and bowls of boiling water were placed beneath. The aroma from this was fantastic and the clothes smelt so much better.

A PROPER CLEAN

To clean your wardrobe properly, take everything out of your wardrobe and either dust it down with a dry cloth or use your vacuum cleaner to go over all the surfaces. Now go over everything with a damp cloth to remove all the dust and dirt. Once this has been done, use a cleaning product, preferably one that is lavender-based (make sure that it has no bleaching agent in it), to freshen up the wardrobe and leave a nice smell.

You must make sure that your wardrobe and rail is completely dry before you put your clothes back in, or staining could occur. It is also worth putting in a perfume bomb to keep the wardrobe fresh.

Drawers should be treated in the same way. Once they are spotless, line them with scented paper. Not only will this make drawers smell nice, but they will also be easier to clean next time around.

tools of the trade

HANGERS

Before you hang your clothes, consider for a moment what type of hanger you use. It is surprising how one can transform a wardrobe by simply hanging the clothes on matching hangers. When opening the wardrobe door, your eyes will no longer be focused on a sea of mismatched hangers all hanging at different levels. Your clothes will now seem to take on a new life and you will start to appreciate them again.

The type of hanger you choose is a lot more important than you may think. The biggest complaint is that most of the hangers listed below are responsible for the dreaded pointy shoulder.

WIRE

I call it the 'heroin' of hangers. This evil contraption may look harmless and your addiction to it may be because they don't take up much room and are free. Think again! Wire hangers easily become distorted, and clothes either hang on for dear life to the drooping shoulders or fall off completely. Another complaint is the coiled wire on the neck of the hanger, which can snag or tear delicate fabrics. Rust can also be an issue, and it is almost impossible to remove from clothes. The long-term damage to your clothes may be irreversible, and there is no rehab that can sort them out.

PADDED

For me, padded hangers are old-fashioned and have no place in a modern-day wardrobe. They also take up too much room, cutting hanging capacity by half. The fabric attracts dust and after time they split and become grubby.

WOODEN

Some wooden hangers are fabulous, but cheap ones often splinter, causing snags and pulls. Clothes also slip off easily if the hangers are highly varnished.

PLASTIC

Multicoloured plastic hangers can be offensive to the eye and look cheap, not doing justice to your lovely clothes. The shapes vary and can be too large or too small. They also snap easily and plastic splinters can occur.

The type of hanger you choose is a lot more important than you may think. The biggest complaint is that most of the hangers listed here are responsible for the dreaded pointy shoulder.

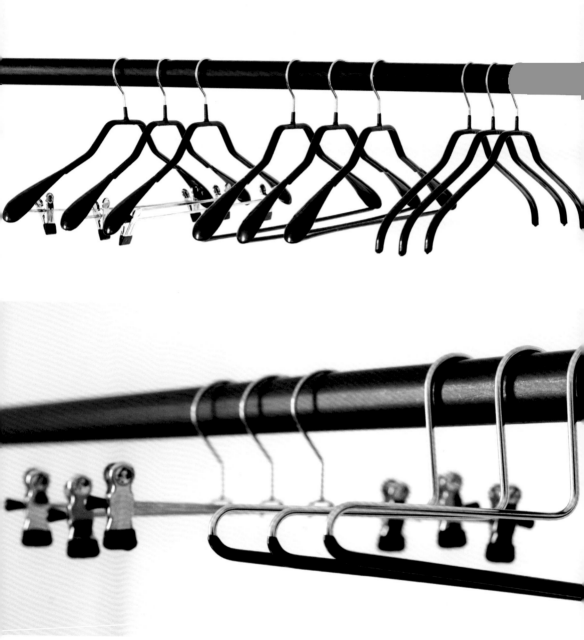

In the same way that your body fits your clothes, so should your hanger. My frustration at the lack of hangers to complement different garments led me to produce my own range. Key considerations for these products were:

• Movable shoulder span
• Non-slip
• Space-efficient and streamlined
• Contemporary
• Unisex
• Unobtrusive colour

I wanted my five-hanger family to sit at exactly the same height, so there would be no undulating effect.

SHIRT
This hanger is the most popular, used for shirts, tops, dresses, knitwear and, increasingly, jackets. This hanger can be gently moulded to the shape of your garment. It is great for knitwear, as it doesn't stretch it.

SUIT WITH BAR
Used for jackets and trouser suits. This hanger has contoured shoulders, so it can be used for most tailored clothing. The trousers should be hung over the bar with the waistband at the back of the jacket.

SUIT WITH CLIP
Designed for skirt suits and for dresses that need extra support, such as strapless or halter-necked evening dresses, for example. Long, heavy evening skirts can also be hung on these. For extra protection when hanging delicate fabrics, put a sheet of acid-free tissue paper under the pegs.

TROUSER
For trousers with a crease, line up the leg seams so that the trousers lay flat, then hang them with the seat pointing towards the open end of the hanger. For jeans and flat-fronted trousers or leggings, fold vertically in half with pockets on the outside (if they have them), with the gusset pointing towards the open end of the hanger. This will create a flat line, giving a uniform look.

SKIRT

Used for skirts and shorts. Before clipping the skirt onto the pegs, make sure any zips or buttons are done up, so that the garment lies flat when hung. These hangers are quite versatile and can also be used for hanging shawls, scarves and even boots. For extra protection when hanging delicate fabrics, put a sheet of acid-free tissue paper under the pegs.

HANGING RAIL

A hanging rail is not essential, but they are so, so useful. You can pick them up quite cheaply and the light, foldable type should be sufficient for your needs. A hanging rail will not only help when you start to reorganize your wardrobe, but it is also useful when you are packing to go away (see pages 122–125).

hanging your clothes by type and colour

To set about the task ahead, you will need to work from the list below. Your garments should already be in sections from when you tried on all your clothes. I now want you to start the process of rehanging and refolding everything in your beautifully clean wardrobe.

Remember that your space is an important criterion; sometimes we can't hang everything that we want to and it may be that, say, jeans will have to be folded, so I want you to start by hanging the non-foldable items. To make this easy for you, the garments to be hung are marked with an (h) on the list below. If you have a garment rail, it will help with the rehanging and colour-coordination process.

- Trousers (h)
- Skirts (h)
- Shirts and tops (h)
- Dresses (h)
- Suits (h)
- Coats (h)
- Jackets (h)
- Knitwear
- T-shirts and vests
- Loungewear

- Resort wear
- Outdoor and sportswear
- Jeans

Take each section, making sure that the appropriate hanger has been used as described on pages 50–55. To be honest, there is no right or wrong direction for your clothes to hang inside your wardrobe – it just comes down to personal preference – but you do need to ensure that all the garments face the same way. This will give your wardrobe a consistent flow.

One of the biggest no-nos is when the hanger hooks face towards you, as this will destroy the streamlined effect you are trying to create. It also takes longer to get your clothes out and you will often find yourself wrestling with the hanger and losing that calm feeling we are trying to achieve.

Now your clothes are hung and sectioned, I want you to colour coordinate them. You will not appreciate the difference this can make until you have seen the result. Put each section into colour groups and then grade them from the lightest to darkest. You will start to see a pattern emerge. There will be link pieces that will help you join the colours together – normally patterned or multicoloured pieces. Don't forget your blacks; textures or sleeve lengths will sit together in this group to give it its own order.

template folding

Whether your T-shirts, vests and sweaters sit on an open shelf or inside a drawer, template folding creates instant order, optimizes space and simply looks better.

You will first need to put your tops into sections – cardigans, V-necks, vests, T-shirts, long sleeves and so on. Once this is done, arrange the garments into colours, usually with the darkest at the bottom. You are ready to start folding.

Place your garment on a clean, flat surface with the front facing down. Now place the template in the centre with the base of the hole at the top of the

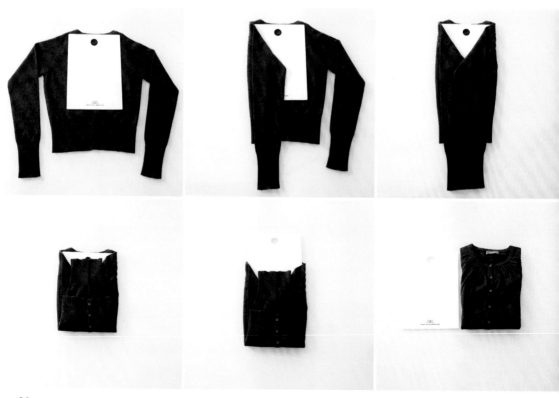

neckline. Fold in the left-hand side and then the right, making sure that any sleeves lie flat with the cuff pointing down to the bottom of the garment. Flip the bottom half up, and if any excess hangs over, fold it in. Gently pull the template out and turn your garment over. After repeating this process on all your garments, you will end up with an immaculate, equally sized pile.

lingerie

Lingerie drawers can be beautiful yet practical. You might think that this is taking organization a step too far, but when time is of the essence and your outfit depends on that nude strapless bra or that sexy lacy set you can't find, you may not think me so mad.

BRAS

Pop the bra cups together, pushing one into the other to create a dome, and then tuck the straps into the back of the cup. Make sure the cups are all facing the same way so that they nest neatly into one another. I prefer to keep bras in the dome shape, as it is more economical on space and great for keeping sets together. Pop the matching knickers behind the cup, then place the bras in straight lines, each one slightly overlapping the one behind, and arranging them by colour.

If you don't like the dome shape, lay your bra flat with the cups facing up and tuck all the straps behind. Any matching knickers can be put behind the cup. As with the domes, make sure you arrange the bras so that they are overlapping and by colour.

KNICKER FOLDING
There is nothing worse than a drawer full of knickers in a tangled mess. Drawer dividers are a great way to prevent this.

Place your knickers down with the bottom facing up, turn in the sides so that the gusset is pretty much even to the sides and then flip the knickers in half. They should now fit snugly into the drawer dividers or behind a matching bra. Alternatively, you can also lay them in the drawer and tier them in colours.

'MIRACLE' UNDERWEAR
'Miracle' underwear doesn't always do what it says on the packet. Bras without straps rarely have sufficient support; decorative nipple guards often highlight rather than hide and seams on control-top briefs, shorts and hosiery can often be unsightly. Be realistic about what you actually wear and edit anything that doesn't work. When you have your 'miracle' must-haves, place them all together so that they are easy to find.

NAUGHTY KNICKERS
If you want to conceal your naughty knickers, put them into satin bags – this will help hide them from any prying eyes and save your blushes! Don't, however, hide them too well in the depths of your wardrobe or drawers, or you might miss out on a moment of passion!

hosiery and socks

My mother is a champion sock folder – you may laugh, but it is true!
Socks were always folded in a flat, neat way. I have taken this
process and adopted it as my own. Here's how she folds them:

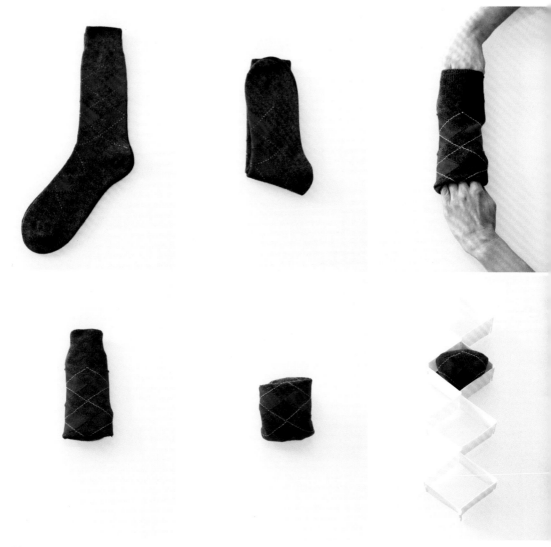

Place the two socks together, making sure that the heels are together, lay them flat and then fold in half. Take the cuff of one sock in your thumb and turn the remaining folds inside out. Your hand should still be inside the socks like a glove puppet. Hold the bottom and, using your other hand, straighten the fabric and flatten the inside folds; you should end up with a neat flat sock.

You can do the same with tights/pantyhose or longer socks. Carry out the same process, but with more folds. By doing this, your socks and tights will sit neatly in a drawer and also fit tidily into a drawer divider.

swimwear

Like knickers, swimwear tends to end up in a tangled mess, with bikini tops and bottoms getting separated from one another. To prevent this, the best way to keep them is in a bikini bag. Before Practical Princess manufactured its own bikini bags, we used ziplock sandwich bags to store swimwear. This is a great way to ensure that all swimwear sits together and the sets stay as a pair.

This system also makes packing for holidays or trips a lot easier. Bikini bags are handy to carry your damp or wet swimwear home from the beach or pool. Remember to take wet swimwear out afterwards though, because if it isn't washed and dried properly, the material could rot or perish.

shoes and boots

We all tend to have our favourite shoes and boots that we wear regularly; usually the same five or six pairs. It is likely that you don't even know how many pairs you own. Even if you are not the next Imelda Marcos, you probably have a lot more shoes than you think, including plenty of pairs that you rarely wear.

I definitely have my day-to-day favourites that I wear all the time, but I also have quite a few other shoes that only work with certain outfits. These rarely get an outing, but I need to keep them close to hand, as they are relevant to my wardrobe and it is important that I can find them quickly and easily.

I don't know how you store your shoes, but I have seen shoes and boots piled at the bottom of wardrobes, thrown under the bed, stacked in old shoe boxes and even scattered all over the house. At some point, most of us have been guilty of this behaviour. But if you keep your shoes like this, damage is certain to occur – anything from your shoes getting squashed and losing their shape to dust becoming ingrained in suede and satin fabrics, or stones and studs getting damaged or lost altogether.

I have learned so much about organizing, displaying and storing shoes by working for Tamara Mellon, the founder of Jimmy Choo. As you can imagine, her shoe and handbag collection is vast. Tamara has over 400 pairs of shoes in her current wardrobe with many more archived, and it is my job to make it easy for her to find any particular shoe.

To do this, I first organize them into style categories. These range from closed toe, peep toe, sandals, wedges, shoeboots, ankle boots, long boots and whatever other style is current. The styles are then colour coordinated and divided into material types – leather, skin, patent and so on. By doing this, any shoe style in a particular texture or colour is easy to find and the visual effect of all the shoes lined up on the shelves creates a boutique-like feel.

Very few people in the world have as many shoes as Tamara and Imelda. I use the same formula for all my clients, but I adapt my system according to what they have. As I do for Tamara, first separate your shoes into categories. Put all your flats together, arranging them in types, e.g. ballerinas, brogues, trainers, flip-flops and sandals. Do the same with your heels. I always keep all my flats on a two-tiered shoe rack at the bottom of my wardrobe for easy access, as I wear them daily.

All my other shoes are stored in Practical Princess shoe boxes with a photo-image on the front produced using our special software. The shoe boxes were specially designed with pull-out drawers because for years it had irritated me that stacked shoe boxes with a lid were impossible to access easily. I always seemed to want the shoes that were right in the middle or at the bottom of the pile of boxes. It was rare that I was able to retrieve them without the stack toppling over and the lids breaking. It would end with me having a temper tantrum and going out in trainers instead!

Shoe boxes are the best way to protect your shoes, especially ones you don't wear very much. I recommend that cardboard is used rather than plastic, so that the shoes can breathe. If you are going to store your shoes in boxes with photographs, then it is a good idea to stack them in categories and colours.

If you want to display your shoes on shelves or shoe racks, make sure that they are dusted regularly. As sad as I may sound, a feather duster does the job perfectly.

For your boots, plastic inserts will help ensure longevity, especially around the ankle. They also enable boots to stand up by themselves.

PRACTICAL PRINCESS

YSL

PRACTICAL PRINCESS

YSL

PRACTICAL PRINCESS

Alexander McQueen

PRACTICAL PRINCESS

Nicholas Kirkwood

PRACTICAL PRINCESS

Cleo B

PRACTICAL PRINCESS

Jimmy Choo

handbags

Like shoes, handbags can get a raw deal. They are often thrown into cupboards, stacked on top of each other or squashed so tightly that the original design takes on a new shape.

I often see handbags being kept in their dust bags, and although this will protect them, the chances of them being used are slim – as they say, 'out of sight is out of mind'.

I have coveted people's handbags and have seen how badly they have been treated. If only there was a 'handbag helpline' and some deserving owner could adopt them (ME!). If you don't want the bag police after you, here are a few tips.

If you visit any fashion website such as Net-a-Porter and look at the delicious handbags they sell, you will see that they have categorized them into a variety of different types: totes, shoulder bags, shoppers, clutches and so on. Different care is needed depending upon the type of bag.

TOTES AND SHOULDER BAGS

I quite often see totes with structured handles being distorted, as the shelves they are stored on are not deep enough. Make sure that the handles have room to stand – if space is limited, the bottom of your wardrobe could be the answer. Stuff the inside of the bag with old newspapers or tissue paper pushed into a plastic bag or dust cover. This will not only maintain the structure of the bag, but it also creates a ready-made removable bag shaper that you can use time and time again.

Most shoulder bags need a bag shaper, but there are a lot of bags around at the moment that are flat in shape. Everybody categorizes this shape differently, but for the sake of argument I will call it the 'shopper'. These don't

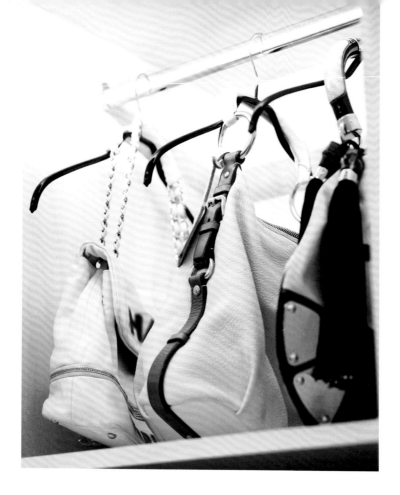

need to have any padding inside and should instead be laid flat or hung on a hook or handle, making a display feature.

CLUTCHES

Clutches come in all shapes and sizes, from the very large to the small and ornate. Shelves and drawers are the best place to store them. If possible, stand them up rather than laying them flat so that you will be able to see them more easily and damage is less likely to occur.

I quite often see handbags being kept in their dust bags, and although this will protect them, the chances of them being used are slim – as they say, 'out of sight is out of mind'.

Stuff the inside of the bag with old newspapers or tissue paper pushed into a plastic bag or dust cover. This padding will not only maintain the structure of the bag, but it also creates a ready-made removable bag shaper that you can use time and time again.

belts

Although I use quite a few different systems for storage, belts give me a headache because there are so many different shapes and sizes around.

You will be able to roll up or coil most of your belts. Keep the buckle on the outside and put an elastic band around the belt to prevent it from unravelling. Arrange your belts by type and colour. Drawers, boxes and trays are all good storage solutions.

Wide belts will vary because of their structure, and laying them flat is usually the best option.

Corset-style belts are structured and need to be stood upright. For a space-saving solution, put coiled belts inside.

Cummerbunds need to be gently folded. Don't use elastic bands to stop them unravelling; if need be, use ribbon.

Another way of storing belts is to hang them. Hooks and belt bars can make a great display feature and are easy to see at a glance. If your wardrobe is deep enough, you can always put these on the inside door of the cupboard, making sure that they will not catch on your clothes.

costume jewellery

I like to see chunky necklaces hung up, as I think they look gorgeous and it stops them from getting tangled, but this is not always practical. If you can, use the back of a door or a small section of wall. You will be able to fix hooks to hang and display your necklaces on. Double and triple hanging will save space and create an eclectic look.

If you don't want to hang your necklaces, an alternative method of storage is to place them in a drawer lined with a piece of suedette or velvet, which should be stuck down – double-sided tape will do the trick. This will stop the necklaces from slipping around and getting tangled up with other pieces.

Rings, earrings and brooches are best kept in jewellery boxes that are compartmentalized. My preference is Perspex trays that are subdivided and that can either be stacked on top of one another or placed inside drawers. Necklaces too can be kept in the same way, but be mindful of tangling. Bangles, bracelets and cuffs are easy to display on a kitchen roll/paper towel holder. Most good homeware stores sell them in a variety of styles.

hats

Hats seem to be the accessories that are often overlooked and forgotten about when organizing your wardrobe. It is worthwhile making them visible or accessible, as hats can totally transform a look rather than just collecting dust at the back of your wardrobe.

The good old-fashioned hat box is still a great way to store the traditional Ascot, wedding hat or fascinator. These are hats that we only take out occasionally, so it is best to keep them boxed. To help you identify them, stick a photograph or label on the box.

Everyday hats, such as a trilby or a flat shooting cap, can be stored on shelves, in drawers or hung from hooks. Baseball caps can be stacked, as can panamas, straws and trilbys. Hats, again, can make lovely visual displays.

scarves

There are so many different types of scarves. The majority can be folded and stacked on shelves or in drawers.

The ones that are usually problematic are the silky types. Some can simply be folded into a square – stack and stagger them so that you can see the different designs. Others, including the fine cashmere and cotton neck scarves that are popular at the moment, can be twisted and bunched to form a ball that can either be boxed or put away in a drawer.

the common clothes moth

Tineola bisselliella, otherwise known as the common clothes moth, is not your average sort of moth that is attracted to light; in fact, they hate it. These little devils are more likely to be found hiding in a dark corner of your wardrobe.

They are small and unobtrusive – only 6–8 mm/⅜ inch in length – with straw-coloured wings and no markings. In fact, they are rather elegant, like a champagne-coloured Concorde! The larvae are creamy white with a brown head and can be up to 10mm/½ inch long. The adult moths don't feed on fabrics, but the female moth lays eggs that hatch out larvae that will feed on your clothes, leaving a tracery of irregular holes. The clothes moth can hide under floorboards, carpets, upholstered furniture, air ducts and antique furniture, and even in felt in pianos.

I've had moths, and if you've had them too, boy do I sympathize! I was verging on an epidemic and am still not quite sure how I got them, but I figure it was through purchasing vintage clothes. If only I had kept them sealed in a bag or taken them straight to the dry-cleaners, I might have saved myself a lot of time and money. I tried all the tips and tricks available, but nothing seemed to work. In desperation, feeling defeated by these evil invaders, I turned to a pest control company to save my sanity and my clothes.

Before they would come to fumigate, I had to dry-clean and launder all the clothes in the house, including sheets, towels, bedding and cuddly toys. You name it, I cleaned it! The whole house was filled with plastic bin liners and boxes, as everything had to be sealed after being washed and dried to prevent further infestation. I actually gave up on what I looked like because it was virtually impossible to get dressed.

After the house was sprayed – which included curtains, carpets and sofas – and I was given the go-ahead to put everything back, I cleaned the house like a woman obsessed. Although financially broke from my huge dry-cleaning and

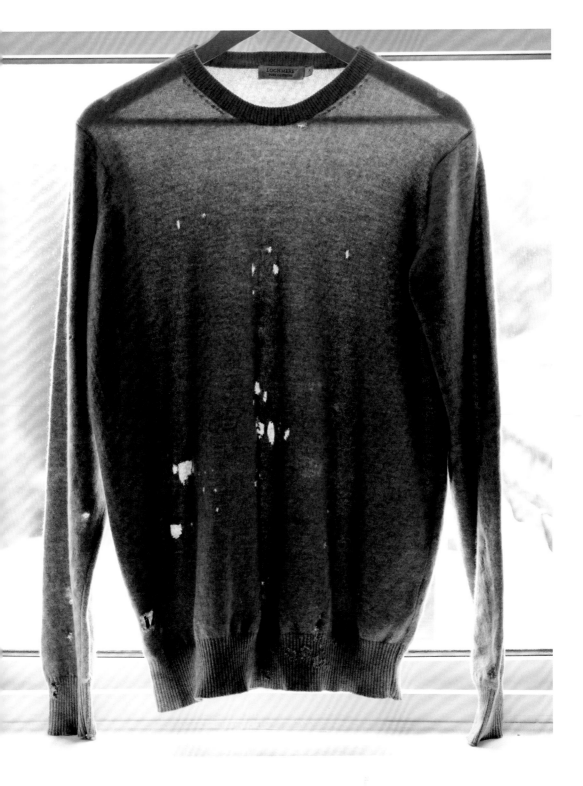

pest-control bill, and exhausted from all the cleaning, washing and ironing, there was a deep sense of satisfaction. I had killed those darn moths, and the house had never been so shiny!

Even though I hope that this never happens to you, I have learned valuable first-hand experience from this drama and it has helped me at work. It has enabled me to tackle moth problems practically and also to understand the emotional impact it has on my clients when these pests attack.

PREVENTION

It is difficult to keep moths at bay, but there are ways of combating them:
- Vintage and second-hand clothing must be cleaned before bringing it home.
- The same goes for second-hand or antique furniture and rugs or carpets.
- Regularly vacuum and clean under beds, skirting boards and furniture.

- Change your vacuum bag often, as this is a breeding ground.
- Clean out the inside of your closet/drawers/cupboards with a bleach-free detergent on a monthly basis (lavender-based products are good).
- Don't put away dirty or soiled clothes. The moths prefer dirty fabric and are particularly attracted to clothing that contains human sweat or other liquids.
- Check and shake garments periodically (lint rollers can help).
- Mothballs are the old-fashioned way of keeping clothes free from moths. However, they are toxic, smell horrid and are unsafe around young children and pets.
- Cedar balls can be effective for the smaller moth larvae, but are not effective for the larger larvae and don't have as much effect as people think.
- Use moth-prevention sachets (including lavender-based products – there are many eco-friendly products on the market).

HOW TO GET RID OF MOTHS

- Dry-cleaning
- Washing clothes in water above the temperature of 50°C/120°F. (I cannot guarantee it, but I have hand-washed things at much lower temperatures and found that this has done the trick.)
- Freezing. This can be used for garments such as cashmere or delicate fabrics that cannot be washed in hot water. Just put the item in a plastic bag and pop it into the freezer for a day.
- Hang items out in bright sunlight. (This might be better for a rug or blankets. I have only used this as a precaution and in conjunction with a lint roller.)
- If you have a really bad infestation, call in the professionals. All companies have different methods of how to combat moth infestation, but most of them use powerful insecticides to kill off the moths.

identifying the gaps

By now, your clothes should be hung in sections and colour coordinated, and as a result, your wardrobe or space will have a very different feel and look. The process that you have just carried out is not just about making your wardrobe look ordered and beautiful, but preparing you for the next stage. By looking at what is left in your wardrobe and cupboards, you should easily be able to identify any patterns such as repeat buys.

When I am working with a client, this is the best time to compile a practical and realistic shopping list. Whether the client is shopping alone or with me, the list will help prevent any impulse buying and constrain magpie behaviour.

When putting your shopping list together, it is essential to keep your wardrobe

assessment in mind and to remember what your goal is. By looking back through your wardrobe, you should be able to identify the gaps.

Do you need any of the following?

BASICS

The cement of your wardrobe: vests, T-shirts, leggings, cardigans and so on, in generic colours (these need to be updated regularly.)

FOUNDATION PIECES

These are the hard-working building blocks of your wardrobe that need to integrate and complement one another in colour. Foundation pieces should include skirts, trousers, jeans, jackets, coats and dresses.

FASHION UPDATE

This could be anything from an accessory to the latest trend in jeans. These items help us to keep our look fresh each season.

LOUNGEWEAR

These are clothes that are comfortable and easy to wear, and that you still look good in, whether you are at home or in the park.

RESORT WEAR

From swimwear to cover-ups, beach hats and sun dresses.

LINGERIE

Strapless bras and seam-free knickers in nude, blacks and whites. The other stuff is up to you!

SHOES AND BAGS

A quick way to update your wardrobe. Make sure that they work for your everyday life. Don't go for the small clutch bag or the pole-dancing shoes that you can't walk in until you have the essentials in place.

ACCESSORIES

A good way to update your wardrobe is with belts, jewellery and scarves, making your look more current.

EVENT WEAR

Something suitable for a wedding, a christening, a day at the races, a glam party, a prize-giving ceremony or even the Oscars to pick up your award!

LINK PIECE

You love it… but you can't wear it because you don't have the right things to go with it.

By identifying what is missing and keeping in mind your lifestyle needs, you should be able to compile a shopping list quite easily. Before you get carried away, you must start with the boring essentials – your basics. No fun, I know – after all, who wants to spend their hard-earned cash on a plain white vest or a black cardigan? It kinda kills that buzz when you get home and empty your bags and there is nothing exciting to show anyone. But, as boring as they may seem, these are the items that are going to tie your everyday look together. Missing or tired pieces from your basic collection can weaken an outfit or sometimes prevent it from working at all.

Foundation pieces are every bit as important as the basics. They are the hard-working building blocks that help to create your style. Essential to your wardrobe, they will be the foundation of your look. They may have a fashion

element, but tend to sit on the classical side. These are pieces that we can wear to death without the risk of being a one-outfit wonder. This is because they can both be worn together and mixed and matched with the rest of your wardrobe.

Each of us will require different foundation pieces to suit our needs. For me and my lifestyle, my foundation pieces will include good jeans that I can wear to work, a couple of tailored and leather jackets, a pencil skirt and a few transitional dresses that will take me from day to night. These items will allow me to dress with ease for my day-to-day life.

Once you have got the staples listed, you can start to add your own touches. These are items that have a personal appeal or fit your own particular style. By adding shoes, bags and accessories or anything else from the list provided, you should have the basis of a well-balanced shopping list.

going shopping

The moral of this story is that you will be more successful when you go out shopping if you look good and feel confident.

looking good and feeling confident

Without wanting to sound like the headmistress of an old-fashioned finishing school, there are some rules that you should stick to when it comes to going shopping. From my own experience, I know that if I look and feel good, I am more successful when I shop. It may not seem important to look your best when you go shopping, but I have witnessed clients having a meltdown when they don't feel confident.

Let me give you an example. I was shopping with a lady for spring/summer wear. Bear in mind that this was mid-February in the UK, right at the beginning of the shopping season.

Like most, after a long winter with covered legs, hers were not looking their best. This made her reluctant to try on dresses and skirts. When she finally did try on a skirt, she sheepishly came out of the changing room. To my horror, she was still wearing her American Tan knee-highs. Not a good look! Luckily, when I pulled up my trousers to expose my pasty pins, she could see the funny side!

The moral of this story is that you will be more successful when you go out shopping if you look good and feel confident. This also applies when it comes to online shopping and trying on goods at home. As obvious as these points may seem, here is a little checklist:
• Wax, shave or depilate your legs and, if you're buying swimwear, do your bikini line.
• If you like yourself with a golden glow, put on a little fake tan.
• If you usually wear make-up, put some on.
• Remember, your hair is your biggest accessory – make it look fabulous.
• Wear good underwear – not your frou-frou lacy stuff, as this will show through clothes, but seamless nude knickers and a strapless T-shirt bra.
• Wear sensible clothes and shoes that are easy to get on and off.
• Wear layers because shops can vary in temperature. There is nothing worse than being too hot or too cold, as it will affect your concentration.

what to take with you

Looking good is not the only key to successful shopping. You will need to take some things with you. I don't want you to be weighed down with bags before you start, but a few things are necessary.

I am not going to ask you to take a pair of high heels with you, as some shops will provide them for you try to on with clothes, or if they don't, you can improvise and stand on your tiptoes.

What I do want you to take are any items that need things to go with them. Trying to remember colours, textures and shapes is impossible, and even with the best eye in the world, the brain can play tricks on you.

Make sure that you remember to take your written shopping list with you. It is all too easy to forget things that you need to buy. Keep your budget in mind, and leave your emergency credit card at home!

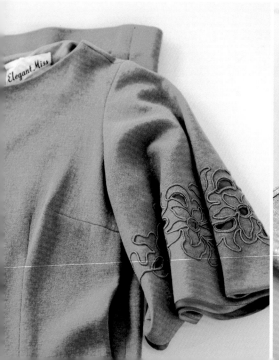

where to go

Where you live and what your budget is will determine where you shop. Your shopping list will also influence where you go.

Shops on high streets, designer avenues, malls and department stores always sit in a cluster. With everything in close proximity and a choice to suit all budgets, this is a great place to start. This is usually the best place to find basics and foundation pieces, so try to do this first rather than leaving them until the end of the day. I cannot emphasize the importance of these pieces enough! Not only will your wardrobe not work without them, but they will

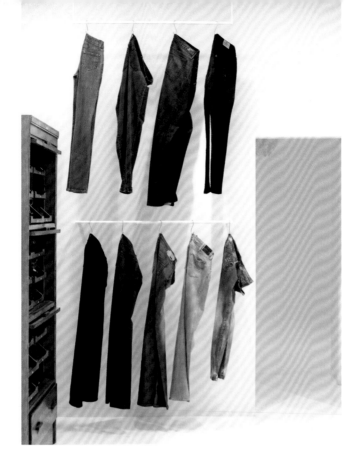

come in useful throughout the day when trying on new pieces. If you blow your budget before you buy these essentials, you will regret it!

Designer jeans brands have exploded onto the market as they have become a must in most women's wardrobes. It is acceptable today even for boardroom executives to wear a pair of jeans with a tailored jacket. Specialist jeans shops have started to pop up everywhere. My personal favourite is Donna Ida in London. Thanks to her large selection of all the latest jeans and encyclopedic knowledge of denim, I rarely need to go elsewhere.

There are other places such as independent boutiques, one-off designer stores and markets where you can pick up unique pieces to personalize your look. Vintage fashion is a great way to get an original look. This trend is so popular and there are many shops around. Some people really suit this style and are good at spotting gems. If this is not your forte, be careful – just because it is vintage doesn't make it cool. You may end up looking like you have raided your childhood dressing-up box!

Designer resale shops are not only there to get rid of unwanted things. They can also be a fab place to pick up a designer bargain. Most shops will only take barely worn or unworn pieces, so you are sure to get a nearly new item at a fraction of the price.

Designer outlets have become more and more prominent in the last decade. From outlet malls to discount retailers such as TK Maxx, reasonably priced fashion is accessible to all. Most of these stores are situated on the outskirts of towns and are not always that easy to get to. If you can't get to one, go online and have a look at theoutnet.com or eBay's fashion outlet. There is a flipside to this sort of shopping – just because something is a bargain doesn't mean that you have to buy it. Do you really need it? Is it on your list?

Sales seem to start earlier and earlier these days. This makes shopping difficult, as it is almost as if we have to buy a season ahead, picking up summer dresses in February and winter coats in August. Unfortunately, unless you shop at the beginning of the season, you might discover that your size is sold out, and find yourself scrabbling through rails of reduced-price clothes and coming out empty-handed. There are of course huge positives to the sales. As they start mid-season nowadays, you are often able to pick up the latest trends and enjoy them immediately at a knock-down price.

If you are at all uncertain about your purchase, it is crucial that you check the refund policies. These vary so much, with some stores not giving refunds at all and only offering a credit note. Markets, vintage stores and second-hand designer shops might not even offer that. You will need your receipt if you want to return an item. A good tip is to keep your receipts in your wallet, not in the shopping bag, to reduce the chance of losing them.

inside the store

This can be really daunting for some people. Clients have explained that when they shop alone everything turns into a blur. The clothes become a mass of colour and items all blend into one. I understand that feeling and have experienced this sensation myself in large stores.

The best way to combat this feeling is to break the space down and pick a small section to start with. Methodically work your way around the shop floor, ensuring that you look at everything in turn, and this will prevent a frenzied supermarket sweep approach.

Most shops are divided into sections and these will be split into fashion stories, designers or garment types. Using the sections as a guide will help to keep you focused and then you won't feel so overwhelmed.

HANGER APPEAL

As you work your way through these little sections, your eye will be drawn to deliberately positioned temptations, quite often on a mannequin. These are meant to lure you in, just as if you were a child in a sweet shop.

Some of these pieces will definitely be worth trying on, but don't overlook the less obvious pieces. Sometimes these items may have little or no hanger appeal, but they will come to life when you try them on and will become the foundation pieces of your wardrobe.

Clothes that are folded will look the same. Take the time to explore these items, as they will inevitably vary in shape and style and you don't want to miss a hidden gem.

the dreaded changing room

Most changing rooms have a policy of six items or fewer and it can be aggravating if you have more than this number of items to try on. The best way to work round this is to logically sort your choices – for example, keep all dresses and jumpsuits together, as they do not require a separate. This will also allow you to compare similar styles so that you find the strongest piece. If you have chosen lots of tops, make sure that you have trousers or a skirt to try them on with.

As you eliminate items, you will be able to bring new pieces into the changing room. Make sure that the attendant knows what you still have to try on, as I have experienced untried items being put back prematurely.

Some attendants are there to give you advice and help you with your decisions. I don't want to give them a bad name, but they can sometimes flatter you into buying something that's not quite right, especially when their commission is on the line.

TRYING ON
Bad lighting, mirrors coming at you in every direction and you have just noticed a new piece of cellulite or flab you didn't realize you had – I am sure we can all identify with this scenario. Braving a shop changing room can be a challenging experience, but rest assured that all women feel the same, no matter how comfortable they are with their body.

I don't want to lecture you on body shapes and sizes, and what will suit you best. There are enough books and magazine articles out there doing this, and I am still not convinced that by following every rule you will get the best results.

One of the things that I have observed from being in changing rooms with my clients is that they tend to stand far too close to the mirror, studying the parts of their body they hate. Ask yourself this question: when you look at someone, do you look at them as a whole or do you zoom in on one particular part? I look at a person as a whole and that is what you need to do too.

When I am shopping with my clients, I am there to be objective, ensuring that the fit and proportions are correct, and that the piece in question is flattering. As I am not in the changing room with you, here's what to do.

Stand way back from the mirror (a couple of metres/five or six feet, if possible), even if this means coming out of the changing room and finding another mirror. Although you may not be comfortable doing this, you have more chance of seeing yourself as others do. It will give you a general overview to see whether the style does suit and flatter.

CONSIDERATIONS

• Are you standing properly? Shoulders back, tummy in, long neck and head high?
• Think about the whole outfit. If you don't have the right shoes, visualize heels by standing on your tiptoes.
• Remember to take off socks or tights/pantyhose if they are not part of the outfit, otherwise it will kill the look.
• Try to be objective and not negative. Do your proportions look reasonably balanced? Or is this outfit/garment cutting your shape up?
• Am I wearing the outfit or is the outfit wearing me? Sometimes less is more.

Having this distance will enable you to see whether the dreaded body part really is that prominent. This can help you change how you perceive yourself.

You do now need to walk closer to the mirror again, but don't stand too close – about a metre/two to three feet away. This is to check the details – to see whether your lines are smooth, and that nothing is pulling or gaping. Sometimes 'miracle' underwear (including bras) can help, so don't forget to wear them or take them with you. Risking it and leaving it to your imagination usually ends in disappointment and a return visit to the shops.

your style

Have you ever wondered how your look or style has been shaped? Our look is not only influenced by fashion magazines, celebrity icons, music and art, but often – without us even knowing it – by our friends and peers too.

Unconsciously, most of us wear a uniform, but not the type we wore at school where everybody looked identical. If you look around the streets, you will notice that groups tend to model themselves on one another. This happens across the board, from teenage girls and boys to pensioners. Of course, some people are completely unique and individual, and stand out from the crowd.

If you want to evolve your look and keep it fresh, here's how to do it:
• When looking through magazines, be realistic – are you looking at the model or the clothes? Place your thumb over the model's face and see if you still like the outfit.
• Strip your look back, playing around with accessories – this is the quickest way to update and change your look.
• Think about your hair – you wear it everyday and it can dramatically change your image.
• Don't be scared to try things on – you might be surprised at what actually suits you.
• Adapt a trend so that you feel comfortable in it – you don't have to go the whole hog and looks can be mixed.
• If the key colours of the season don't suit you, you can always wear them away from your face or as an accessory.
• Don't overlook make-up, because this can really change a look, as can eyebrows and skin tone.
• Less is more. If in doubt, keep it simple – minimalism is always a success.
• You don't have to stick to one look. Have fun with clothes – fashion changes and so can you!
• Project your personality through your style.

shopping for special occasions

This can be one of the most stressful types of shopping. No matter how long we have to prepare, we often end up leaving it to the very last minute.

Special occasion outfits are usually a one-hit wonder. The formality or the dress code limits what we can wear, and we want to look our best. Whether it's for a christening, a wedding, the races or the party of the year, special occasions are when we often become impulsive and lose our senses. Try not to do this, as the item you buy will inevitably end up not being worn again. Instead, aim to be more timeless in your choices: block colours and simple clean lines tend not to date and are more versatile. Build a look with accessories: hats, gloves, jewellery, shoes and handbags.

Going to the hairdressers for these events can make you feel a million dollars. Hairpieces can really add drama and glamour as well, but make sure that the person who is doing your hair is experienced. A spray tan and professional make-up will also help create that wow factor. When I need extra assistance for special events, I use a London-based company called InParlour, as they come to my home and save me valuable time. I have also used the in-store make-up services at MAC and various other cosmetic companies in the past.

My top tip for having professional make-up applied is to always start with a more natural look. The worst thing is staring at yourself in the mirror and not recognizing your own reflection. It is important to feel comfortable and confident. Remember, it is easier to build a look up than to try and tone it down.

packing

We all have different packing habits. Some of us will pack a week or two in advance, while others will still be packing when they should be on their way to the airport. Both of these approaches have their downfalls. If you pack your bag too early, you may find that you forget what you have put in and throw in unnecessary extras. Favourite items that you have packed but then want to wear leading up to your holiday will be pulled out of your case. But chucking everything in a case at the last minute means you will almost certainly pack too much or too little. Nothing will go together, and the creased and mismatched items will give you a unique holiday look!

BE PREPARED
The destination and length of your trip will determine what you need to pack. Lay out in advance what you think you will require and what you would like to take. Think about how many outfits you will realistically need and make sure that each outfit can be completed by mixing and matching. Don't forget to lay out lingerie, sleepwear, sportswear and so on – you would be surprised how easy it is to forget these items. You may find that you have put out far too much. We all do it. Be realistic and go back over your choices to decide what you actually need. A garment rail can be very useful during the process: you will be able to assess how well your holiday wardrobe works together.

If you need to cut back on accessories, metallic shoes, handbags and belts are a great way to lighten the load, as they tend to go with most colours.

Think about the time of day you will arrive and what you will be doing when you get there. Set aside what you will first need to wear – a bikini for the beach, for example, a ski suit for the slopes or pyjamas for bed. These should be packed at the top of your case for easy access when you arrive. This will stop you rummaging through your perfectly packed case and creasing all your clothes.

HOW TO PACK

Make sure that everything is clean and pressed before you start. A square wheelie case is preferable because the rigid sides reduce the chance of creasing. Lay the more structured clothes flat at the bottom – the fewer folds, the better. Use tissue paper to separate and protect your clothes from other items that can scratch or damage them. Once these are all in, you can pack your next layer. This will be the foldable items like T-shirts, jeans, shorts and so on. Fill any spaces with small items such as socks and underwear to create a solid base for your next layer. Shoes should be bagged and placed around the edges of the case, and bulky items such as handbags, toiletries, leather jackets and waterproofs can then be placed in the middle.

I like to take the majority of my toiletries and cosmetics in my hand luggage, but many airlines impose security regulations when it comes to carrying liquids onto the plane. If in doubt, check with your airline, as it is infuriating having your favourite perfume confiscated when going through security. When it

comes to toiletries, do try not to buy up the chemist shop/drugstore before you leave. You can always stock up at the airport or when you arrive.

UNPACKING

The last thing most of us want to do when arriving at our destination is unpack our suitcase. Here's where that little bit of preparation really comes into its own. You are ready to go and can grab whatever you need from the top of your case, leaving the unpacking until later.

This does not mean that you can leave it until mid-holiday. It is important to unpack as early as you can so that any creases can drop out. If you find that certain items look like a well-weathered face, hang them in the bathroom so creases can drop out in the steam.

index

credits

The author and publisher
would like to thank the
following designers,
boutiques and businesses
for their help with
photography for this book:

Lucy in Disguise
10–13 King Street
London WC2E 8HN
020 7240 6590
www.lucyindisguiselondon.
com
*Pages 2, 85 right, 96 above
left, 105, 107, 112, 113,
114, 117*

Donna Ida
106 Draycott Avenue
London SW3 3AE
020 7225 3816
chelsea@donnaida.com
www.donnaida.com
Pages 106, 109, 111

9 London
www.9london.co.uk
*Dress from 9 London on
page 16 above left*

Philip Treacy London
69 Elizabeth Street
London SW1W 9PJ
+44 (0) 207 730 3992
studio@philiptreacy.co.uk
www.philiptreacy.co.uk
*Hat by Philip Treacy on
page 86*

Agent Provocateur
www.agentprovocateur.com

La Senza Lingerie
www..lasenza.co.uk

Jimmy Choo
www.jimmychoo.com

Net-a-Porter
www.net-a-porter.com

Topshop
www.topshop.com

Anthology Boutique
511 Old York Road
London SW18 1TF
07947 467385
anthology@live.co.uk

**Make-up by Amanda
Harrington @ InParlour**
www.inparlour.co.uk
020 7736 7713
info@inparlour.co.uk

Hair by Darren Hau
07979 081522
darrenhau@hotmail.com
Celebrity, session, catwalk,
photographic, TV

**Kynance Dry Cleaning
& Laundry**
2–3 Kynance Place
London SW7 4QS
020 7584 7846

Portrait on page 12 by
David Daughton

The publisher would like to
thank those who kindly
allowed us to photograph
their wonderful homes and
wardrobes, including Emily
Evans and Grainne
Stevenson. We also wish to
thank our models, Alex,
Anna, Clare, Darren, Emily,
Karim and Maddie.

acknowledgments

There are so many people I need to thank for their help and assistance in getting this book to print, but Maisie, my beloved daughter, has to come top of the tree. Seeing the way she has fought her own battles since a baby and the achievements she has made has given me the strength to fight on when I felt that things were not going to plan. I am so proud of her – thank you, Angel.

I must then thank my mum, who has been the biggest role model in my life. Her hard work, love and determination have inspired me. She is the 'Practical Queen'. I must also thank her for the hard work she put in on the book. My dad, Poppie, must also be thanked, for always believing in me and instilling in me the belief that there is nothing I cannot do.

What would I have done with out the help of my assistant, Anna Hitchins – a truly talented young lady. She has worked tirelessly beside me, though tears and laughter, compiling this book. Thank you Anna – you are a star!

I would also like to thank my cousin Debbie and my wonderful friends, especially Hannah Coleman, Gilly Smith, Emily Evans, Maddie Farley, Waggi and Simon, who have had to listen to numerous readings and have helped me in so many ways. The list goes on, but I must not forget Grainne Stevenson, Claire Arden, Angie Robinson, Olivia White and Victoria Stephenson.

I would also like to thank Tamara Mellon, because of her faith in me and for all her help with Practical Princess.

To all at RPS a big thank you, especially Alison Starling for approaching me and giving me the opportunity to write the book, Annabel Morgan for being kind about my writing ability, Leslie Harrington for allowing me to use my own creative visualization and Polly Wreford and her assistant Sarah for such beautiful photography and interpreting my vision.